Isaac Gregory Smith

Characteristics of Christian morality : considered in eight lectures preached before the University of Oxford in the year 1873

Isaac Gregory Smith

Characteristics of Christian morality : considered in eight lectures preached before the University of Oxford in the year 1873

ISBN/EAN: 9783337263478

Printed in Europe, USA, Canada, Australia, Japan

Cover: Foto ©Lupo / pixelio.de

More available books at **www.hansebooks.com**

THE
BAMPTON LECTURES
FOR 1873.

"It has come, I know not how, to be taken for granted by many persons, that Christianity is not so much as a subject of enquiry; but that it is, now at length, proved to be fictitious. . . . . . On the contrary, ... any reasonable man, who will thoroughly consider the matter, may be as much assured as he is of his own being, that there is not however so clear a case, that there is nothing in it."—*Extract from Bishop Butler's Preface to his " Analogy of Religion."*

Characteristics of Christian Morality.

CONSIDERED IN

EIGHT LECTURES

PREACHED BEFORE THE UNIVERSITY OF OXFORD,
IN THE YEAR 1873,

ON THE FOUNDATION OF THE LATE

REV. JOHN BAMPTON, M.A.

CANON OF SALISBURY.

BY THE

REV. I. GREGORY SMITH, M.A.

LATE FELLOW OF BRASENOSE COLLEGE, OXFORD;
VICAR OF MALVERN, AND PREBENDARY OF HEREFORD;

Author of "Faith and Philosophy," "Epitome of the Life of Our Blessed Saviour," "Fra Angelico and other Poems," &c.

Oxford and London:
JAMES PARKER AND CO.
1873.

EXTRACT

FROM THE LAST WILL AND TESTAMENT

OF THE LATE

REV. JOHN BAMPTON,

CANON OF SALISBURY.

———

——— "I give and bequeath my Lands and Estates to the
"Chancellor, Masters, and Scholars of the University of
"Oxford for ever, to have and to hold all and singular the
"said Lands or Estates upon trust, and to the intents and
"purposes hereinafter mentioned; that is to say, I will and
"appoint that the Vice-Chancellor of the University of
"Oxford for the time being shall take and receive all the
"rents, issues, and profits thereof, and (after all taxes, re-
"parations, and necessary deductions made) that he pay all
"the remainder to the endowment of eight Divinity Lecture
"Sermons, to be established for ever in the said University,
"and to be performed in the manner following:

"I direct and appoint, that, upon the first Tuesday in
"Easter Term, a Lecturer be yearly chosen by the Heads
"of Colleges only, and by no others, in the room adjoining
"to the Printing-House, between the hours of ten in the
"morning and two in the afternoon, to preach eight Divinity
"Lecture Sermons, the year following, at St. Mary's in
"Oxford, between the commencement of the last month in
"Lent Term, and the end of the third week in Act Term.

"Also I direct and appoint, that the eight Divinity Lecture Sermons shall be preached upon either of the following Subjects—to confirm and establish the Christian Faith, and to confute all heretics and schismatics—upon the divine authority of the holy Scriptures—upon the authority of the writings of the primitive Fathers, as to the faith and practice of the primitive Church—upon the Divinity of our Lord and Saviour Jesus Christ—upon the Divinity of the Holy Ghost—upon the Articles of the Christian Faith, as comprehended in the Apostles' and Nicene Creeds.

"Also I direct, that thirty copies of the eight Divinity Lecture Sermons shall be always printed, within two months after they are preached; and one copy shall be given to the Chancellor of the University, and one copy to the Head of every College, and one copy to the Mayor of the city of Oxford, and one copy to be put into the Bodleian Library; and the expense of printing them shall be paid out of the revenue of the Land or Estates given for establishing the Divinity Lecture Sermons; and the Preacher shall not be paid, nor be entitled to the revenue, before they are printed.

"Also I direct and appoint, that no person shall be qualified to preach the Divinity Lecture Sermons, unless he hath taken the degree of Master of Arts at least, in one of the two Universities of Oxford or Cambridge; and that the same person shall never preach the Divinity Lecture Sermons twice."

TO THE

REV. EDWARD HARTOPP CRADOCK, D.D.
PRINCIPAL OF BRASENOSE COLLEGE, OXFORD,

THE

REV. SAMUEL WILLIAM WAYTE, B.D.
PRESIDENT OF TRINITY COLLEGE, OXFORD,

AND THE

FELLOWS AND SCHOLARS OF THOSE COLLEGES

These Lectures

ARE INSCRIBED.

PREFACE.

THE pressure of other duties, of which I had no anticipation when I undertook the Lectureship, has compelled me to modify the original plan of these Lectures. This may be some excuse for their faults.

I hope that others will do more effectively what I have here attempted. The moral features of Christianity are an essential part of its evidences, especially for the requirements of our time.

Among the friends to whom I am indebted for assistance kindly given I have especially to thank the Rev. J. B. Mozley, D.D., Regius Professor of Divinity, Canon of Ch. Ch., Oxford, and the Rev. Phipps Onslow, M.A., Rector of Upper Sapey, for valuable suggestions in revising. If I have omitted acknowledging any obligation to previous writers, it is an oversight which I regret.

The intelligence of the death of Mr. John Stuart Mill arrived while these Lectures were being delivered. I trust that, in essaying to reply to some of his opinions, I have never been unjust to one whose candour and earnest desire to be impartial command the respect of those who differ from him.

I. G. S.

MALVERN,
May 31, 1873.

LECTURE I.
WHAT IS MORALITY? 1

LECTURE II.
VIRTUE IS UNSELFISHNESS: VICE IS SELFISHNESS 15

LECTURE III.
CHRISTIANITY AND THE APPETITES . . 33

LECTURE IV.
CHRISTIANITY AND AMBITION . . 49

LECTURE V.
CHRISTIANITY AND SELF-DEPENDENCE . 63

LECTURE VI.
THE UNIVERSALITY OF CHRISTIAN MORALITY 77

LECTURE VII.
ALLEGED DEFECTS OF CHRISTIAN MORALITY . 87

LECTURE VIII.
SUMMARY AND CONCLUSION . . . 99

APPENDIX . 109

LECTURE I.
What is Morality?

ISAIAH xxiv. 18.

"*The foundations of the earth do shake.*"

FOR good or for evil, in these days of ours, nothing is taken for granted. Creed, system, institution, all must justify their existence. No prescription however venerable, no authority however sacred, may plead exemption. The restless tide of thought washes away the accretions of ages; the convulsive heavings of doubt and enquiry lay bare the hidden principles of belief; "the foundations of the round world are discovered;" "the foundations shake;" "the foundations are cast down." Surely for good in the end. Many a stately edifice, the pride of generations past, comes crashing down, because reared on shifting sand, "and great is the fall thereof." But that which stands on the rock will stand unshaken, while all else is reeling and tottering around.

So, then, Christianity must be prepared to prove itself. For Christianity is simply nothing, unless it is reasonable and voluntary. Only a debased and sentimental Christianity would say, "Feelings are better than reasons, and render reasons unnecessary[a]." Christianity claims no inert acquiescence,

---

[a] "People are accustomed to believe, and have been encouraged in the belief by some who aspire to the character of philosophers,

no servile prostration; it appeals emphatically to the conscience. It must stand or fall by this criterion,— Is it founded on the sand or on the rock?

I propose in these Lectures to consider the morality of the Gospel as an evidence for the doctrines of which it is the accompaniment; nay, of which it is the substructure and the foundation. Religion without morality is a body without a soul. If the ethical teaching of Christianity, fairly tested, is superior to that of other systems, here is one of the surest arguments, if not the very surest of all, for Christianity as a whole: and the argument is strengthened, in proportion to the degree of superiority.

I need not remind you who hear me, that, outside the pale of numbers[b], proof positive and irrefragable, is simply not to be had; and that the most we may dare to hope for is but a balance of probabilities. If moral and religious truths admitted of demonstration, their influence as a probation and discipline of character would not be what it is. Need I implore you also to bear in mind the axiom, more than ever needful where the question is so wide in its range, so momentous in its issues, that the justice of the cause must not be gauged by the inadequacy of its advo-

---

that their feelings on subjects of this nature" (rules of conduct) "are better than reasons, and render reasons unnecessary."— J. S. Mill, *On Liberty*, p. 4.

[b] If the value of words and their relation to one another could be defined as exactly as in numbers, to the exclusion of all irrelevant matter, the inference logically drawn from them would be, as an inference, demonstrable.

cate; an inadequacy of which he is himself only too well aware.

Are we over-stating, if we call morality the foundation of religion? Surely no. "By their fruits ye shall know them," are the words of the Founder of Christianity; and the test holds good, as of His disciples, so of His doctrine, and, with reverence be it spoken, of Himself. For what is Faith? Not the dry apprehension by the intellect of barren formulæ, but a willing appreciation of what is beautiful and good, and a trustful surrender of self to one worthy of love and reverence. What is there blameable in Unbelief[c], but the wilful rejection of truth and holiness? Or, to be more exact, since all believe in one thing or another, the difference lies in the object of faith. There is a gradation from the lowest to the highest faith; from the faith of mere materialism, a faith, as it has been called, "in man's digestive powers and in the Everlasting Nothing[d]," up to the loftiest conceptions of Almighty Holiness and Love.

This connexion between faith and morality, between worship and common things, is an especial mark of Christianity. In other religions, with which we are familiar, the daily life was slightly enough affected by creed or ceremony. The Greek or the Roman might go his way from altar or temple,

[c] The unbelief which comes from circumstances, either within the man or without, for which he is not responsible, is essentially different from the unbelief which comes from the will being warped by any selfish prepossession.   [d] T. Carlyle.

satisfied that having poured his libation, or suspended his votive offering, he had done all that his gods could require. But from the first the key-note of Christianity has been, not hands cleansed by lustral ablutions, but hearts pure from taint of evil; not the praises of the lips only, but a life devoted to what is good. Inconsistency there is, of course, among Christians, as elsewhere; and this proneness to relax the obligation, to put asunder what God has joined, is encouraged now-a-days by a vague and unreal way of speaking, as if morality were something different from what is termed spirituality[e], something of a lower sort. Still, be the faults of Christians what they may, Christianity promulgated itself as a new morality, though not as a morality only; it marched over the earth, "conquering and to conquer," with "Love to God, Love to Man," blazoned on its banner; even its more abstract doctrines, if not merely gazed at from afar, but realized by an experimental sympathy, and assimilated into the believer's being, are an inspiration of the highest morality[f]; and, by consent of all, the truest Christianity is there, where the life and the creed are most truly in accordance. To many minds, if not to all, the moral loveliness of the Gospel is a stronger

[e] S. T. Coleridge has remarked that the word "Spirit," "as a power or property seated in the human soul," never occurs in the New Testament but in context with some moral quality.—*Aids to Reflection*, p. 42.

[f] One of the most obvious illustrations of the connexion between morality and theology is in the Manichean rejection of the doctrine of the Incarnation.

proof of its truth than any manifestation of power, however stupendous.

But here we are confronted by the question, old as the Sophists [g], yet ever new,—What *is* morality? We are told of an almost infinite, quite irreconcilable, diversity of opinion about the rules of right and wrong. "No two ages," it is said by a great thinker of our own day, "and scarcely two countries, have decided the question alike; and the decision of one age or country is a wonder to another [h]." It may be. But rules are not principles. Rules of morality may vary, as laws, customs, languages vary. But to argue from this diversity of rules that there are no fixed principles of morality would be as reasonable, as to argue from the difference of dialects that these have no common origin, or from difference of inflexion or of syntax, that there are no grammatical principles at all. Races of men, like individuals, may be predisposed especially to this or that virtue, repelled especially by this or that vice. The hardy Scandinavian, the versatile Greek, the subtle Hindu,

---

[g] Cf. Arnold's *Thucydides*, vol. iii. Pref. xxi.

[h] Mr. J. S. Mill, *On Liberty*, p. 3. It may be noticed, however, that Mr. Mill, after saying "what these rules" (of conduct) "should be, is one of those" (questions) "in which least progress has been made in resolving," yet allows in the context that we must "*except a few of the most obvious cases.*" This is an important limitation. Mr. E. B. Tyler speaks similarly of "the shifting rules by which men have divided right from wrong."—*Primitive Culture*, ii. 97. In other parts of his able and almost exhaustive book he speaks of the "moral standard" even "in savages," (as, indeed, it is in children,) being "real enough, but far looser and weaker than ours." (i. 27.)

the dull Hottentot, may have each his own idea of
what constitutes a hero, each his own idea of a fool
or a knave. Particular periods in history may canon-
ize one moral quality, may proscribe another. One
generation may look too leniently on the inordinate
pursuit of wealth; another on the inordinate pursuit
of military glory. Even at the same moment, within
the four corners of the same territory, may coexist
side by side almost contradictory standards of moral
excellence and of moral depravity, according to the
prejudices of different classes in society. Notions of
morality vary with the varying predispositions of
time and place, of circumstance and temperament.
Nay, the immediate impulse may vary. An Italian
may be swayed by sentiment chiefly; a man of more
phlegmatic, less æsthetic habit, by a sterner sense of
duty[1]. But all this does not prove that there is
no fundamental consent under these discrepancies.
The manner of applying rules of action to particular
cases may vary almost endlessly; the rules themselves
cannot be stereotyped independently of contingencies
which may arise; but the great principles of truth,
purity, kindness, are as undisturbed by these vicis-
situdes, as the depths of the Atlantic by the storms
which ruffle its surface. The moral sense of even
the wisest and best of men is fallible[j], for he is but

---

[1] Cf. J. S. Mill, *Inaugural Address to the University of St. Andrew's*, Feb. 1, 1869, p. 43.

[j] "The fallibility of what is called the moral sense."—*J. S. Mill,
On Liberty*, p. 5. The "*odium theologicum* in a sincere bigot," which
Mr. Mill cites in the same sentence "as one of the most unequivocal

one. The collective voice, if not of all humanity, yet of the humanity most worth listening to [k], speaks with no faltering voice. To this we make our appeal, "Judicet orbis terrarum!"

How this sense of right and wrong comes to be what it is, is no part of our question. We need not pause to ask, whether it is an heirloom from the remotest past, or the product of a progressive evolution from savagery to civilisation, just as, to borrow an illustration [l] from an able writer on civilisation, the sextant is developed from the mediæval astrolabe, or the needle-gun from the obsolete matchlock. On the likelihood of this or that hypothesis we may have an opinion, and a strong one. But the question itself is hardly practical. Man, it has been well said, with all his rare endowments, is what he is,—a being

> " with such large discourse,
> Looking before and after;"

be his lineage what it may; even as the athlete or the philosopher, with all his developed symmetry of limb or intellect, was once an embryo in the womb. So conscience is, what we feel it to be,

---

cases of moral feeling," is simply a case of a *diseased* moral feeling, so far as it is really hatred. So far as men in persecuting others for their religious tenets have believed it "the only way to save souls," the error, however deplorable, is an error of judgment rather than of the moral sense, an error not about the end in view, but about the means to it.

[k] Cf. Aristotle's appeal to those only who are competent to speak —οἱ πεπαιδευμένοι (*Nic. Eth.*, I. iii. 5).

[l] E. B. Tyler, *Primitive Culture*, i. 13.

a voice claiming to direct, to urge [m], to restrain, even were it as certain as it is problematic, that conscience had its beginning in blind instincts of mere utility [n]. Even could it be shown, that our conceptions of what we call right and wrong originated in some mere physical convenience, and have only by slow transmission from age to age attained their matured strength as bonds of society, still the fact remains—they are here, they are among us, they are within us; in thrilling tones heard above the storm of passions, they assert, not their existence merely, but their rightful sovereignty over us and our actions. What matter whether conscience, yearly, daily, hourly, expanded itself and ripened, as from the feebleness of infancy, or leapt into being at the Creative Word, full-grown and panoplied for the strife of passions, like the virgin-goddess of Athens? Questions like these, as unnecessary for our present purpose as they are interminable, may well be left on one side. We take our stand on what is, not on

[m] Mr. J. S. Mill strangely narrows the office of conscience, by regarding it mainly as "negative," ... "with most men a power chiefly in the way of restraint,—a power which acts rather in staying our hands from any great wickedness, than by the direction it gives to the general course of our desires and sentiments." *Inaugural Address to the University of S. Andrew's*, p. 43. This is, indeed, to bring against "the conscience of most men" the same very grave accusation which Mr. Mill elsewhere (*On Liberty*, p. 29) brings against Christianity, of attending to the passive duties of life to the neglect of those of an active kind.

[n] The fact that expediency and right as a rule coincide in their consequences, is no proof that right is based upon expediency. "Honesty is the best policy;" but, it has been well said, "the man is a knave who acts on that motive."

what may have been. We appeal to the normal conscience of civilisation.

What, then, do we mean by morality? Only the relations of man to man, or his relations also to a power above himself? We may not exclude these latter altogether. It will be said, that we are importing alien matter into the argument; nay, that we are begging the question. Not so: we do not assume, in so doing, the truth of this or that theology, nor even that there is any truth in any theology at all. We argue simply from what we see and know; we take theology as exhibited practically in its bearings on life and character. Nor are we importing anything extraneous; for there is a mutual action and reaction of morality and theology; each is largely shaped and coloured by the other; nay, so inextricably are they blended, that you cannot sever them without violence to both. To men of different creeds duty has not the same meaning. The man who does not believe in a God, or, what is in fact the same thing, does not believe that he knows anything about Him, is a foundling on the earth, without a tie to parents whom he has never known. The man taught that his gods are cruel, false, licentious, indolent, or capricious, is a son whose father's example conflicts with all that is noblest in himself°. The man who

---

° ποῦ χρὴ τίθεσθαι ταῦτα, ποῦ δ' αἰνεῖν, ὅταν
τὰ θεῖ' ἐπαινῶν τοὺς θεοὺς εὕρω κακούς;
      Soph., *Phil.*, 451.

Compare Horace's theology (*Sat.* I., v. 101) with its practical result (*Epist.* I., vi. 1).

For the Pagan idea φθονερὸν τὸ θεῖον, see the story of Polycrates

looks up to a just, pure, beneficent Deity has, in love and reverence for Him, the strongest incentive to justice, purity, benevolence. Even though the actions may seem to coincide, the motive-principle does not; and motives, not actions, are the business of morality. Therefore, while we fix our attention chiefly on morality as ruling the relations of a man to himself and to his fellows, we may not in fairness close our eyes to the relation in which he stands to his God.

But we are asked what we mean by *Christian* morality [p]? and we are told that the morality of one sect is not that of another. True, speaking superficially. A Scotch Covenanter, for instance, and a Spanish monk of the Inquisition may easily be drawn so as to present very different types of morality. But while the points of contrast stand out from the surface, the points of identity are, if we look within, deeper and more real. This at least will be granted. If we find a principle of conduct which is a common feature in the several groups, so strangely, sadly sundered, of the Christian family, not peculiar to one period, one race, one school of thought, one set of conditions,—this is Christian morality. The fatalism of the Calvinist, —the fear of God which seems almost to "cast out" the love of God in Puritanism,—the austerity, the blind submission to authority of Monachism, may belong severally to a one-sided development of Christianity. But the love of enemies, the forgiveness of injuries, are duties recognised in theory, if not always

---

of Samos (Herod., *Hist.*, iii. 41), and the speech of Artabanus to Xerxes (*Ib.*, vii. 10). [p] J. S. Mill, *On Liberty*, p. 28.

in practice, by Christians everywhere. We need not go to chapter and verse in Gospel and Epistle, nor to the sayings of Saint and Doctor, however eminent; but we take the pervading dominant intention of the records of Christianity, and the essential moral unity of Christendom. Even in the words of Him who is the Truth, who "spake as never man spake," we look in vain for an elaborated code of rules, or even of principles. It is indeed here, in the life and teaching of Christ, that we find the fullest embodiment of our morality; if, that is, we realise that He was indeed made "like unto us in all things," and that His being "without sin" was not immunity from temptations, but a triumph over them; if, instead of imagining Him while He walked the earth clad in armour of proof against evil, something between God and man, like the demigod of antiquity,

"Too fair to worship, too divine to love;"

we realise that He laid His glory by for our sake, and was indeed God made Man. It is in Christ Jesus that we see the "Beauty of Holiness[q]." Still, it cannot be too often repeated, He came not to found a school of philosophy, but to live and die in entire self-sacrifice for others. His life on earth contains the germs of all that is good, as the seed-vessel contains the fruit and flower; but it is a suggestion, not a demonstration of what we ought to be; that men should learn not a parrot-lesson of performing certain

[q] For the present argument it is enough, if the Gospel narrative is accepted as authentic in its outlines of the character and teaching of Christ.

acts, but a habit of willing with a certain intention; should become good, not merely do good things.

So, then, let us take morality in its fullest sense, as embracing not only what man owes to man, but what he believes himself to owe to a higher power, so far as this affects his human relations. Let us mean by morality those fundamental principles of right and wrong, which are of general, if not absolutely universal, acceptance. Let us understand by Christian morality, the standard of morality generally accepted among Christians. In attempting our comparison of the Christian morality with that of other systems, let us be careful to discriminate between what is essential and what is accidental, between what is of general and what of only particular application, between what is really distinctive of a creed and what is not. On the one hand, we must not impute to Christianity any moral excellence previously existing in full vigour, any amelioration really due to some other cause,—for instance, to nationality or to the progress of civilisation. On the other hand, we must deduct from the claims of systems posterior to Christianity, whether at Rome [r], Alexandria, or Paris, what they owe to the Christian atmosphere which they breathe, to the unacknowledged influences of the very discipline which they repudiate with scorn. Let us measure a system, not as it may have been caricatured by its opponents, but as it is seen in its best specimens; not contrasting, as has been done, John Knox with Pericles [s], nor, as we might

[r] See Note A.   [s] J. S. Mill, *On Liberty*, p. 361.

be tempted to do, Nero with St. Louis of France. Let us mark not the highest types only of a morality, but the average level of its proficiency; not so much the one or two solitary achievements of a system, as its results ordinarily; not merely what it has aspired to in theory, but what, though only too often thwarted and baffled by human frailty, it has actually done. Above all, may the Spirit of Truth, the Spirit of Love, guard us from unjust disparagement of what is really honourable, wherever we may meet it; guard us from stinting or grudging our praise to those who deserve it, whether friends or foes of the faith which we cherish. Bow down we must in lowest reverence before the only faultless holiness which the world has ever seen; but let us hail with thankfulness the scintillations, faint and broken though they be, which attest in all times and in all places the never-ceasing struggle of light against darkness, and which converge from saint and sage in every quarter under heaven, to weave a crown of glory for the brows of Him who said, "I am not come to destroy, but to fulfil."

LECTURE II.

Vice is Selfishness: Virtue is Unselfishness.

ST. MATTHEW x. 39.

" He that loseth his life for My sake shall find it."

THAT morality is not a name, but a thing; that a comparison may fairly be drawn between the morality of the Gospel and the morality of other systems; and that the truth of a creed is evidenced by the soundness of its morality; so far we have advanced already. Bear with me, if I ask you to pause yet on the threshold. The more cautiously we move at first, the surer, and swifter, too, will be our progress in the end.

We want a clear conception to start with, of some one essential principle of right and wrong. Granted that there is such a thing as duty or responsibility; that the word "ought" is not a mere expletive in our vocabulary;—still, we have to ask the limits and the nature of this responsibility. How far is man responsible for his conduct? And what is it that makes his conduct right or wrong?

It may, I suppose, be taken for granted, that, just as in our ordinary speech the adverb is the most important word of the sentence, so the conditions of an action qualify it as good or evil; that responsibility begins and ends within the bounds of possibility, or, in other words, that an action must be judged according to what is possible in the circumstances; that the act of doing is more important than the thing done, if for no other reason, because productive of a moral habit the parent of many similar actions; that the action is, as it has been well expressed, but the clock-finger of the process going on within a man; that, in short, morality is to be found in the intention, not in the act. All these are axioms which are not of yesterday [a]. We see and feel, besides, what may be termed a strong family-likeness in the category of the virtues which the moralist approves and commends, and something of the same deformity in the vices which he reprobates. Any kind of fault, if unchecked, seems invariably to lead on to others, which might even have been thought diametrically opposite. The tender-hearted man becomes hard as a flint, in the gratification of his lust. The man who is scrupulously just becomes unjust to others under the spell of rancour and animosity [b]. Morality, in fact, like everything else, must be taken as a whole; it is no aggregation of anomalous precedents; it obeys a law; it is quickened by a living principle. What then is it, which underlies the manifold forms of what we call morally right and wrong, and gives to each its being?

[a] Arist., *Eth. Nicom.*, I. vii. 14; I. x. 13; I. vi. 15.
[b] Similarly, there is a close inter-dependence of virtues, at first sight unconnected, e.g. of courage and purity.

We must have recourse to psychology. There is no need, happily for us, even to set foot on that mysterious domain, where the transcendentalist

"Finds no end in wandering mazes lost."

But, while questions of ontology, of the existence or non-existence of time and space, and so forth, are far removed indeed from any practical bearing on our question, psychology is as real and practical a study as any other; and to the moralist it is indispensable. For how can questions about man's responsibility be answered, without first defining what he is? And this we must attempt to do, avoiding, so far as possible, technicalities of expression.

Let us frankly concede, at once, to materialism, all that is not really tenable. As physical science extends its researches, it seems scarcely to admit of question, that much in our composition which has hitherto been vaguely regarded as immaterial and spiritual, is really the direct result of certain operations in our physical organization, which are as mechanical as the revolutions of the wheels in a watch. But in this concession we are not for one moment surrendering the great, and, as I most firmly believe, the inexpugnable truth of man's free-will, of man's responsibility.

That which differentiates man from the brutes is not the faculty of reasoning, — for they reason too, and what we are pleased to call instinctive sagacity is often our own inductive process in its lowest, homeliest form. Nor yet is it our emotive nature,—for even our nobler qualities, fidelity or courage, for instance, find their counterpart in other creatures. It is this. While the dog apparently knows not whether he is faithful or faithless, and the elephant reasons to all appearance without any consciousness of his cleverness, man is introspective, —is able to detach himself from himself,—is always, more or less explicitly, sitting in judgment on himself, passing sentence on himself, awarding to himself praise or blame. In brief, man is conscious.

So, then, let us regard the personality of each one of us as co-extensive and identical with this consciousness of willing. Granted, that our moral sentiments are not intuitive, not innate; or only innate, as the invisible writing, which cannot be deciphered without being held to the fire, or as the characters, wellnigh obliterated, of a palimpsest. Granted, that the most complicated concatenations of consecutive thought may all be resolved into the bare perception that this and that are like or unlike, identical or not. Granted, that the many-tinted play of the emotions may all be analyzed into a mere liking or disliking for this or that object presented by the senses immediately, or mediately by the intellect. But the life, the personality of each resides in his individual consciousness. All else, even within the man, is but as the dress which he wears, the apparatus with which he is equipped, the dwelling assigned to him for his sojourn. His faculties, of intellect, of emotion, are not himself. He is a machine, if you will; but a machine with a living person continually ad justing, directing, controlling it; and that person is himself.

This way of regarding human nature, as it accords with the investigations of modern science, is also essentially in accordance with Christianity. So long as we suppose that a man's intellectual ability or feebleness, his emotional tastes or distastes, are himself, rather than something belonging to him, for the use or abuse of which he is responsible, so long a grave difficulty must remain, for those who believe in a future state. This strange disparity, which we see around us on every side, of mental and moral endowments, how is this to be reconciled with our belief in an identity of existence which survives the grave? Must not the inferiority of capacity, which is a clog and a hindrance here, be a clog and a hindrance hereafter? But once let us grasp the idea, that the faculties, intellectual and moral, of a Shakespeare, say, or of a Plato, are like his money, or his dress, or his bodily health, a part of what he has, rather than of what he is, a property entrusted to his keeping, more to one, and less to another, like the talents in the parable, in every case to be made the most of—then we can understand how the street arab from the Seven Dials, who starts in the race of life so grievously weighted, or the peasant who plods along with disqualifications in their own way as serious, may, if they do their best, find themselves one day on a level with the philosopher and the statesman, who have lived and died faithful to their high calling, and this, without ceasing to be themselves.

It may be said, that in thus surrendering to materialism so much of our being, we are opening the door to the surrender of all; tracing on the sand an arbitrary line, which the next wave of scientific progress will efface with its touch. Not so. We are merely exchanging an untenable position for one which is proof against assault. We draw the line between matter and spirit, where conscious volition commences; and the distinction is no arbitrary, no merely theoretical one. It is founded on a fact, which is, I think, generally admitted. Will any one say, that a man is responsible for the images, fair or foul, which flit across the retina of his intellect, except so far as he allows these or those to linger there? Or for the desires within him, noble or ignoble, crying out to be appeased, except so far as he gives ear to the one or the other? It is because he prefers, because he selects, because—two courses lying before him—he lets himself be drawn to the worse or the better, because by a supreme and irrevocable fiat, an inheritance from his Creator, he pronounces his deliberate decision, that the idea figured to his conception by the brain, and urged by all the eager advocacy of the heart, is to be consummated into action, and, because in so deciding he knows that he is deciding for good or for evil, herein is his responsibility.

But all this, we are told, is exploded. The will acts, it is allowed, "in accordance with motive;" but to suppose that the will can "break loose from continuity and act without cause" is as absurd, it is added, as to suppose "a balance sometimes acting in the usual way, but also possessed of the faculty of turning by itself, without or against its weight [b]." But we do not say that the will is "acting without cause;" for the will itself is an item in the causation; nay, to omit the will is to omit the most important factor in the calculation. We do not say that the will is "breaking loose from continuity," for the will itself is a connecting link in the chain of continuity. With contending motives equal, as sometimes happens, a man would be as powerless to stir one way or the other, as the ass between the two bundles of hay, but for the intervention of the will. Even with one motive, to all appearance and by all laws of experience outweighing the other, the will, simply by its own adhesion, can reverse the balance. The tender maiden chooses rather to endure the rack or the dungeon, than succumb to the torturer. The veteran confessor for his faith frustrates all the hopes of his disciples by preferring shame to suffering. The scales are adjusted; the weightier motive, be it of a better or a worse sort, an appetite, an ambition, a self-devotion to some unselfish cause, is sinking down; the lighter kicks the beam; but the will, like the victorious Gaul, flings its sword into the scale, and all is changed in a moment. True, the weights in these scales have no fixed intrinsic value, but one which varies subjectively to each of us. Even causes external to us, hereditary predispositions, early influences, local asso-

[b] E. B. Tyler, *Primitive Culture*, i. 3.

ciations, all must be counted in. True, habitual indulgence may give to a propensity a force not its own, may even make it, by long persistence, a tyrant of that to which it should be a servant and an instrument. True, the will may become so enfeebled in its miserable thraldom that only by an extraordinary effort can it be free. Still, after all, the final verdict in that little court, where each man presides, arbiter of his own actions, of his own happiness, is not in the power of any propensity or inclination, but rests with himself, and resides in the conscious energy of his will[c].

One part of our question is answered. But what is it which makes this exercise of volition good or evil morally?

The whole universe, real or phenomenal, it matters not for our present enquiry how we style it, if considered from the stand-point, at which we have arrived, of each man's personality, resolves itself for him into self and nonself; and the faculties, mental and moral, already spoken of, are, through the instrumentality of sense, the media of attraction or repulsion between the world without and the smaller world of each individual existence. Here, then, we have a principle, wide as the range of our conceptions, simple as all first principles are, determining the moral character of all that we do, say, feel. When the individual, using his faculties as a prehensile instrument, draws the outer world to himself, there—in one shape or another, in greater or less degree,

[c] See Note B.

disguise it, deny it, as we may—there is selfishness. When the individual, by the same media of communication, lets himself be transported out of himself, and drawn to the world without, there is the opposite of selfishness, call it what you please, self-devotion, self-renunciation, unselfish love, charity. "Drawn," you will say, "to something evil—can that be virtuous?" Stay. To say that a man is drawn to anything vicious, is simply a loose and inaccurate way of speaking. The pure, high-minded artist is drawn to the beauty which he worships. The voluptuary, the miser, the tyrant, are stamped as vicious in this, because they are, each and all, absorbing into themselves the world around them, to glut their insatiable cravings for pleasure, wealth, power [d]. *Things* and *persons* [e]. In these words is a practical touchstone for us and our motives. The ideally vicious man recognises no personality but his own. Outside himself all is impersonal. Others exist only as things for his pleasure or convenience [f]. On the other hand, the unselfish see everywhere in the world around them the claims, not to be slighted, of beings like themselves. Self seems as nothing in presence of all these manifold demands on their sympathy. Far from regarding their fellows as inanimate chattels, the world to them teems with the sacredness of life. In the noble words of one, from whom I find myself some-

---

[d] St. James, *Epist.* iv. 1; cf. Carlyle, *French Revolution*, bk. ii. ch. viii. p. 49. [e] The idea is, I think, Bentham's.

[f] The wickedness which takes account of other personalities only to torture them is a monstrosity.

times compelled to dissent, they feel "the miserable smallness of self,—the poorness and insignificance of human life, if it is all to be spent in making things comfortable for ourselves and our kin, in raising ourselves and them one step higher on the social ladder [g]."

This is no mere theory. Take any statute-book that you please, from the Sinaitic decalogue to the latest codification of modern legislators. The things forbidden,—murder, theft, adultery, and their cognates, spring from self disregarding the rights of other personalities, and into this are resoluble. Pass from overt acts to the virtues and vices of moralists, —cruelty, lust, deceit, what are these but self caring only for self, and closing its eyes to the existence of others as persons. Or take those two widely-divergent, mutually-abhorrent affections, which we, as if the inconsistency of our hearts must brand itself on the mintage of our lips, class together under the homonym of love, desecrating the highest attribute of humanity—the love which is indeed hatred, for it would make a holocaust of the happiness of those whom it professes to cherish, to feed the devouring flame of its own passion—and the self-immolating love—it is no poet's dream, it can be, has been, is— which "holds its life but as a pawn" for others, and which, in the Apostle's fervent words, would even wish itself "accursed" to secure another's happiness. Are we not justified in saying, that

---

[g] J. S. Mill, *Inaugural Address at St. Andrew's University*, p. 44.

selfishness and unselfishness, the bane and the antidote, grow side by side at the very root of all within us which we term good and evil [h]?

But, it must be kept in mind, this self-abnegation for the sake of others is no suicidal frenzy, no self-annihilation, no absorption of self into the soul of the universe. For what in that case would be left for love to live for, to energise upon? Obviously, unless the result is to be an utter vacuity of inanition, each one is bound to observe the law of self-preservation, for this very reason, that he may live for others; is bound to look to his own interests, that he may live for others more effectively. Nor is this limitation incompatible with the purest disinterestedness. The motive makes all the difference. If a man saves, that he may have to give to those who need; or economises health and strength, that he may work longer for others; or studies self-culture, that he may better play his part in life's drama, not to catch the plaudits of the audience, but to carry out the glorious conceptions of the great Designer,— he will do more good to others in the end, than by reckless almsgiving, or by defiance of hygienic laws, or by shuffling through his part on life's stage, because it is his own. Here is the "gulf" that is "fixed"

---

[h] Contrast St. John xiii. 34, "A new commandment I give unto you, That ye love one another; as I have loved you, that ye also love one another," with

ὡς πᾶς τις αὑτὸν τοῦ πέλας μᾶλλον φιλεῖ,
οἱ μὲν δικαίως, οἱ δὲ καὶ κέρδους χάριν.

Eurip., *Med.*, 86.

between faith and fanaticism. Both have the same motive principle. Both give up self for others. Faith is reasonable, and takes account of the means indispensable to the end. Fanaticism is blind, and despises them. Here, in this due adjustment of what have been called our centripetal and centrifugal forces, is that harmony of love and order which the artist sighs for. Moralists have spoken of inordinancy as that which vitiates affections innocent otherwise, or even laudable[1]. But it is not the amount of energy bestowed which makes them wrong, it is the motive which lurks at their core. The highest ideal which we can imagine of goodness and greatness is surely this, entire self-devotion for the good of others as the motive power, with wise regard to every consideration which can in any way be made to subserve this end.

One word more, before we apply this cardinal principle to our enquiry. It may be objected, even by those who admit man's free-agency and his responsibility in volition, that we are, after all, only substituting one kind of selfishness for another; that the man whose motive is love, is really pleasing himself as much as he who thinks only of his own ease, advancement, self-improvement; that, in brief, he is doing what he likes best. The objection in one sense neither admits of any answer, nor requires one. Of course, every exercise of the will implies a choice and a preference. It is a tautology, a truism to say so.

---

[1] "Strong impulses are perilous only when not properly balanced."—*J. S. Mill, On Liberty*, p. 35.

The will selecting what it does not like best is an impossibility, except indeed, which is virtually no exercise of the will at all, under constraint of a physical necessity. So far no answer can be, need be given. But how is the will to be brought into this state of cheerfully surrendering the things dearest, because nearest, to itself for the sake of others? By no short nor easy process. Even in those who are most happily constituted the preparatory discipline is a work of time and toil; of stern battling with desires and appetites. I will not say it is a constant crushing down of rebellious cravings, for the unselfishness which we are speaking of is not that dreary silence of human affections which some call peace[j], but a harmony of all their voices; it is a constant "keeping them in subjection[k]." Wisest and holiest can tell us, if we ask of them, that the attainment of perfect unselfishness is, like the artist's pursuit of ideal beauty, a life-long striving towards an ever-receding goal; it is self victorious over self; it is self victor and vanquished in one.

It will be my endeavour in subsequent lectures to apply this criterion of unselfishness to Christianity.

But we are asked, how we dare to claim this as a specialty of Christianity, we who have seen rising before our eyes a system which protests against Christianity as selfish, and boasts itself more pure from self-love; a system which, though an exotic in England, yet approves itself to the thoughts and

---

[j] "Solitudinem faciunt, pacem appellant."—*Tac.*, *Agric.*
[k] 1 Cor. ix. 27.

usages of a civilization, such as we have arrived at, and is at this moment not without an indirect practical influence in this country?

Now, before meeting the charge of self-seeking advanced against Christianity, it must be premised that "Altruism" is itself an offspring and a product of Christianity. Whether, indeed, Altruism could ever have been but for the fostering care of eighteen centuries of Christianity, and whether it can exist in any vigour apart from Christianity, may fairly be doubted.

But, waiving this, let us look more closely at what "Altruism" means. What is its motive and its mainspring? I think we shall not be doing an injustice to the Positivist, if we say that his "Altruism" means doing good to another, because this will be the good of all. But this is by-no-means tantamount to saying, "Do well to others, because it is their due." Prudence or amiability may make it easy for any one to confer benefits which will redound to the good of all, the benefactor included; but a reciprocity of favours like this, a co-operative partnership for mutual advantages, is something different from the teaching of words like these, "He that loveth his life shall lose it; he that loseth his life for My sake shall find it."

Let it be noticed, besides, that in proposing love for Himself as the motive to His disciples, Christ is proposing a yet higher motive than love for our fellow-creatures. And this for two reasons. First, because the object proposed is more truly worthy of love. Next, because the sincerity and the reality of love are then most tried and proved when it is for one unseen, and apprehended only by an effort of thought, even as the remembrance of an absent friend is a better proof of love than constancy to one whom daily associations make it almost impossible to be unmindful of. So far, I think, it will be allowed that Altruism falls short of the motive which Christ proposes to His disciples: "Bear all, do all, be all for My sake[1]," and "that men may glorify your Father which is in heaven[m]."

But exception is taken to the promises of the Gospel: "He that loseth his life shall find it." And to this I must ask your patience while I devote to it a little space, before I conclude.

Let all be conceded that in fairness ought to be. Yes. The Gospel of Christ does hold out a hope of future retribution; does enforce its precepts with a blessing and a curse,—with a promise of great reward, with a threat of severe punishment. Still, even if it must be granted that what has been called "other-worldliness," is really a modified form of selfishness, and that those whose motive is only the hope of heaven, the fear of hell, are in their own way as selfish as the miser or the voluptuary, are not really "lovers of that which is good," let us pause before we believe that a creed which again and again reiterates the great principle of

[1] St. Matt. v. 11; x. 18, 22, 39: St. Mark viii. 35; xiii. 9. 13: St. Luke vi. 22; ix. 24; xxi. 12, 17: St. John xiii. 38; xv. 31.
[m] St. Mark v. 16.

self-sacrifice can belie itself by encouraging a mercenary spirit in its adherents. That some believers in Christianity allow their thoughts to dwell too much on its prizes and penalties, that we are all in danger of doing so, is no fault of Christianity, unless, indeed, Christianity puts these things first and foremost. This can hardly be affirmed. They are always there, these hopes and fears, in the Gospel of Christ, but they are in the background of the picture. The "outer darkness" reserved for the unholy, far from casting its gloom over all the canvas, is shrouded by a veil of mystery. The mansions of the blest are only seen faintly and far away, like the distant hills of the promised land seen by the seer on Pisgah. Again and again Christ warns those who would follow Him, that they must "count the cost [n]" of what they are doing; that they must nerve themselves to take up the Cross, to bear the Cross without a murmur as He bore it up the slope of Calvary, to immolate upon the Cross the self-love which hinders perfect self-renunciation, even as He offered Himself upon it. If Christianity ever seems to allure its disciples by its promises, to scare them by its threats, it is but as an earthly parent, well-knowing all the time that virtue, unless sought for its own sake, is not virtue, yet strengthens the native weakness of purpose in his child, by wise apportionment of praise and blame, of reward and punishment, till the lesson has been learned, so hard to learn rightly, that, though duty and happiness are

[n] St. Luke xiv. 28.

one, duty must always be sought first, without even a sidelong glance at consequences.

Above all, the nature of the reward promised must be considered. It is distant, and therefore cannot be grasped even in thought without that "patient continuance in well doing," which is the only test, the only discipline of a resolute will. It is unknown, and therefore can have no charm except for those, who, in the trustfulness of love, cast themselves on His Word, whom they believe to be too wise, too true, too loving, to deceive them. It is not merely unlike vulgar notions of happiness, but contradictory of them; no prolongation of earthly joys, but a transfiguration of them; and therefore it appeals to those only who act from conviction. It is not the hireling's coin, grudgingly worked for, grudgingly paid down, but a gracious Master's approval of willing service,—no bait to attract half-hearted votaries to swell His train,—no vision of sensual joys or of earthly dominion,—it is only for those, who, in renouncing all that the selfish deem life worth having for, can find outside themselves the happiness which they have not sought. For

"Love is Heaven, and Heaven is Love."

LECTURE III.

Christianity and the Appetites.

GALATIANS v. 24.

"*They that are Christ's have crucified the flesh with its affections and lusts.*"

IF, in accordance with principles indicated in previous lectures, we are to test a system of morality by the position and attitude of self to the world without, it will be convenient to classify the emotions: for through these the individual is attracted to, or repelled by, the objects of which he is cognisant; by these he is moved to draw them to himself or to repel; while, as has been said already, in the assent which the will in each instance consciously gives or withholds, the essence of morality resides.

Without pretence of philosophical exactness, it will be enough for practical purposes, if we adopt an old threefold division of the emotions, according to the various objects on which they are exercised. There are the bodily appetites, as they are called; there are, what may be called, the desires of personal aggrandisement; there are the desires, in regard to which, in a stricter sense than usual, self is at once centre and circumference, which end, as they begin, in self, which seek their consummation in a serene abstraction from external things. Thus the great typical temptations of the Son of Man[a] ascend progressively from the lower appetites, and from the desire of earthly dominion, to the selfishness of self-dependence.

Obviously, in this enumeration the appetites of the body are the lowest; they are common to man with the brute; common, among men, to the coarsest organizations with the finest. Not that vices of this class are of necessity the worst. On the contrary, if a comparison must be made, and if the old saying, "corruptio optimi pessima," is true, the perversion of higher impulses is yet more fatal to moral excellence than a grosser kind of depravity. Caliban, with all his brutality, moves our pity even more than our detestation. The sensuality of the brute-man is not so hideous as the fiendish malignity of Mephistopheles.

How, then, does Christianity deal with these appetites of the body?

It would be idle to set about proving that Christianity preaches temperance and purity. If there have been here and there in history fanatics who have sullied the name of Christianity by "turning the grace of God into lasciviousness[b]," they are too exceptional and too inconsiderable to be noticed. Equally futile would it be, and most unjust, to attempt to deny, that these same virtues have been inculcated outside the pale of Christianity. Glowing panegyrics on sobriety and purity, grave cautions against excess, lofty aspirations after the repose and

[a] St. Luke iv. 3—12.   [b] St. Jude Ep. 4.

serenity which wait on appetites subdued, may be quoted from the precepts of Greek and Roman philosophers, or of Oriental mystics. It may be possible even to find a parallel elsewhere to what is more distinctive of Christianity, its earnest and repeated warnings on the necessity of being pure in thought as well as in deed, of guarding the secret well-springs of intention from pollution. If the Gospel teaches, "Blessed are the pure in heart [c]," and "He that looketh on a woman to lust after her hath already committed adultery with her in his heart [d];" so Buddhism teaches that it is wrong even to think, in regard to a married woman, that her husband is a fortunate man [e]; so the Roman satirist [f] tells us, that the man who meditates a crime is guilty of the action.

Where, then, is the difference? It is here—in the motive, which is the life and the essence of the precept. Of all the passages which might be culled from the Christian Scriptures on this subject, the words in the text seem to declare most emphatically the Christian's motive for temperance and purity. "They that are Christ's,"—so writes St. Paul to his converts in Galatia—"have crucified the flesh with its affections and lusts." Ye are Christ's,—here is the

---

[c] St. Matt. v. 8.

[d] St. Matt. v. 28. Mr. F. W. Newman calls this "an extravagant and obscure way of speaking."—*Defective Morality of the New Testament*, p. 25.

[e] I cannot recollect in what writer on Buddhism I found this statement.

[f] Juvenal, *Satir.* xiii. 209, 10; cf. Herodot., *Hist.*, vi. 86.

motive; and, because ye are no longer "your own," but His, who died for you, therefore your affections and lusts, being a part of the nature dedicated by you to Him, to whom you owe everything, must be "kept under and brought into subjection [g]," even as He for your sake subjected Himself to the death upon the Cross. Christianity regards our human nature as identified with the divine in Christ; "Ye are members of His Body, of His flesh [h]." "Shall I then take the members of Christ and make them the members of a harlot [i]?" Christianity regards the human body as a shrine for the presence of Christ by His indwelling Spirit. Our mortal bodies are "temples of the Holy Ghost [j]." How, then, can we desecrate what Christ in His love has hallowed for Himself? Others may tell us of the injurious effects of intemperance to health of body and of mind, of the misery which it entails, of its degradation. But Christ would have us temperate, not so much from calculation of consequences to ourselves; not so much with a view to our own comfort and convenience; not so much even from respect to the dignity of our nature, as because intemperance is a detraction from

---

[g] 1 Cor. ix. 27.   [h] Ephes. v. 30.
[i] 1 Cor. vi. 15. Mr. F. W. Newman, in his ingenious but unpractical essay on the *Defective Morality of the New Testament*, represents St. Paul as "propounding chastity only as a spiritual or transcendent duty, binding therefore on the saints but not on common men," (but "saints" was the designation of Christians generally,) and proceeds even to argue that, according to the Apostle's teaching, fornication with a Christian woman would not be sinful [!]. (p. 24.)   [j] 1 Cor. iii. 16.

that willing service which we owe to Him, a breach of our allegiance, a faithlessness in our love.

The comparative feebleness of other motives is attested by results, as "the tree is known by its fruits." Motives of self-interest are as powerless to quell the insubordination of the appetites as the "seven green withs" of the Philistines to bind down the son of Manoah. For if it is due merely to myself, if I owe it to myself alone, this temperance, I am debtor and creditor in one; nor can any one gainsay my right to relax the obligation, if I please, or even to cancel it altogether, giving myself a full and free acquittance. If, with my eyes open, and seeing what the end of the bargain must be, I still choose to squander the happiness which is my birthright for a passing gratification, who shall complain, for, who is wronged? But if I am bartering away what is not mine but another's, the health and strength which ought to be expended in His service to whom I am bound by every tie of gratitude and love, if I am prostituting affections which are of right His alone, then I have a motive which can quench the fire within, if anything in the world can. A Cicero or a Seneca may descant on the charms of temperance, on the folly and baseness of excess; but the impotency of their eloquence is evidenced not by one, or two, or three vicious emperors only, but by the wholesale debauchery of an Empire. The founder of Buddhism may hold up to the eyes of his disciples a dazzling vision of the grandeur of a superhuman mastery over the senses, of a godlike isolation of the spirit from the material world, but the myriads of India are the slaves of an impure superstition. The Koran may enjoin temperance, but Mahometanism is a byword for sensuality. Even the sterner morality of the Mosaic law cannot command obedience, or emancipate man from the tyranny of himself. It was "a schoolmaster to bring men to Christ[k];" but the appetites were unruly pupils. The ceaseless and reiterated rebukes of the prophets, in the later days of the national existence, are but an inevitable sequel to the old story of Israelitish contact with Moab, of Israel's wisest, greatest kings seduced by fleshly lusts from the self-control which they could extol, but could not practise. Nothing short of that passionate yet stedfast devotion to Christ, which is the answer of the soul to His self-sacrificing love, and which the Apostle speaks of as "constraining[l]" us, can keep down these volcanic forces, for ever making havoc and anarchy in our nature by their wild upheavings.

What can be more attractive at first sight, or, so far as it goes, more compact and complete, than the teaching of Epicurus? Virtue is the highest pleasure, the only true happiness. Be virtuous, and you have all that you can desire. But the charmer charms in vain. Men will not see it; or, rather, they will accept the half of his doctrine, and refuse the rest. Pleasure shall be their end; but not such pleasure as he proposes. They will seek happiness, as he bids them, but not in his way. Thus the amiable self-love, so like benevolence to a hasty glance, which the

[k] Gal. iii. 24.   [l] 2 Cor. v. 14.

master taught, soon degenerates in his scholars into mere sensuality; the optimist's acquiescence in whatever is, becomes a languid indifference to improvement; the artistic love of beauty becomes an idolatry of the senses; and the followers of one whose ideal happiness was virtue, as if transformed by the wand of the enchantress, grovel in the mire, and devour greedily the husks of a momentary self-indulgence. For the motive, if not radically wrong, is inadequate and incomplete. The mainspring is wanting. Self-love must be dethroned; and in its place must stand One worthy of entire self-devotion.

But has Christianity succeeded in this apparently hopeless undertaking of reducing the flesh to submission, and of evoking harmony out of its discordant cries? Are there no sins of the flesh among Christians? Alas! these vices have been in every age a reproach to the "pure religion and undefiled[m]" which we profess. Still, let this be remembered; these vices have never dared among Christians to assert an undisputed sway. In every age, and not least in our own, Christianity has originated heroic efforts to cope with a gigantic evil; efforts which serve to hold the foe in check, if not to dislodge him from his position. The carnality, which assimilates itself with other creeds so readily as to become soon an integral part of the ritual and of the daily life, has always been a glaring enormity among Christians; a thing protested against unremittingly; a plague-spot, the very sight of which suggests con-

[m] St. James i. 27.

tinually new remedies, new preventives. If our great cities teem with solicitations to drunkenness and unchastity, is there not an army in array of noble-hearted men and women, such as no other religion can show, ever at work with their manifold organizations, as well as with the yet stronger persuasiveness of a holy example, to remove the reproach from among us? And what is it that nerves the soul in this never-ceasing conflict with evil? It is no sordid calculation of results to self; nor is it even a nobler regard only to the welfare of our fellows and to the prosperity of our country; but, above all other motives, it is that "love of Christ[n]" which believes that it can never do enough for His sake who has done all for us, and which rejoices in so believing.

Besides, as no other motive can so effectually subdue the lusts of the flesh, so no other motive, paradox though it may sound, can hold the balance steady, when by a recoil in its oscillations the pendulum sways from sensuality to an undue distrust and dread of the senses. The longing for purity becomes in Buddhism a panic-stricken loathing of all that is material, nay, by an insensible step forward, of life, of existence altogether. The thirst for rest from the unworthy importunities of our animal nature can only be slaked by the utter annihilation of the individual. And, (need I remind you?) the very intensity of this yearning to be enfranchised from the bondage of the flesh often drives the soul in its despair to the recklessness

[n] 2 Cor. v. 14.

of the grossest materialism. Often, the more sublime the upward soaring, the more headlong the fall of the soul, unless upborne by a strength not its own, by the power of love. For if the motive of our strivings after purity be of a merely selfish kind, a wish to be independent of the troublous fluctuations of the material universe, to be self-poised and self-contained in a sublime tranquillity, then what limits shall be set to our endeavours, day by day to live more completely aloof from the contamination of matter, more and more ensconced within a world whither the illusions of the senses cannot enter? The goal recedes ever before us. But if, in our endeavours to be pure, we are acting not for ourselves and by ourselves, but for Christ and by Him, then we shall regard matter, not as a defilement to our touch, but as a thing to be handled with care and reverence in His service; and our senses, not as of necessity traitors to us in our dealings with the outer world, but as emissaries whose communications are to be received with caution, not rejected utterly, and the desires of our lower nature not as foes to be exterminated in an internecine warfare, but as mutineers to be brought back to their allegiance to their king. For, to abhor the material world, the senses, the affections of the body, is to abhor the agents and the instruments which are all to be dedicated to His service.

Perhaps it will be objected, that Christianity itself has engendered a morbid asceticism, as extreme and as unreasonable as can be found anywhere. Are not Simeon on his pillar, Antony in his cave, the monks of La Trappe in their cells, worthy to be ranked with the self-torturers of India? But let us examine the parallel more closely. Monasticism, even if we take the word in its widest sense, as embracing both the solitary life and the cœnobitic, though widely prevalent among Christians under certain conditions, is no integral part of Christianity, but an excrescence, an abnormal product of local and temporal circumstances. Monasticism was originally provoked by the fury of persecution, and by the seemingly hopeless corruption and misery of the society by which Christianity in its infancy found itself environed. And whenever the flickering, dying flame of monastic ardour has been re-kindled in subsequent ages, it has been as an exceptional and extraordinary protest against luxury and indifference. Monasticism, if considered dispassionately, not with the blind partizanship of those who welcome it as the most potent agency for consolidating the power of the Papacy, nor with the blind intolerance which sees in it a manifestation of Antichrist, must be allowed to have its merits. To some it has been, and these not a few, a shelter for souls wearied out by the storms of a turbulent age; it has attracted others by offering them a more thorough devotion of their lives to the Saviour's service. But it is not the offspring of Christianity, as the names of the Essenes and of the Therapeutæ testify; it is no specialty of the Church, as the name of the Encratites reminds us; it can only justify its existence under the Gospel by appealing to a text here, and a text there, divorced from the general tenor of the Gospel message. In short, whatever may have been its services to religion, monasticism fosters the notion that there is merit in making life more miserable than it need be; it implies a dereliction of active duties, and an abhorrence of matter strangely at variance with the life and doctrine of Him, who "came eating and drinking º," whose first miracle was wrought at a wedding-feast ᴾ, and of Apostles who learned from Him "how to use the world as not abusing it ᑫ," and how for His sake to "become all things to all men ʳ."

Take marriage for instance. See how Christianity, while vindicating the lawfulness and the dignity of marriage against the disparagement of an ecstatic asceticism, guards it from degenerating into the legalised licentiousness of polygamy or concubinage. Christianity takes the animal passion, and ennobles it. "Marriage is honourable," it says, "and the bed undefiled; but whoremongers and adulterers God will judge ˢ." Where else is the marriage-bond riveted with so firm yet tender a hand, or hallowed by a sanction so inviolable? A man is "to leave" (even) "father and mother, and" (to) "cleave to his wife;" and "what God has joined, no man" is to "put asunder ᵗ." Elsewhere, the wife is often a thing to be bought and sold, a part, and not always the most precious of the husband's chattels, or, at best, his companion for a time in a partnership "lightly

---

º St. Matt. xi. 19.   ᴾ St. John ii. 2—11.   ᑫ 1 Cor. vii. 31.
ʳ 1 Cor. ix. 22; cf. 1 Tim. iv. 3; Col. ii. 16—23; Rom. xiv. 14;
Tit. i. 15.   ˢ Heb. xiii. 41.   ᵗ St. Matt. xix. 5, 6.

enterprised," and as lightly sundered. In Christianity the tie, once accepted, is all but indissoluble, and its mutual responsibilities are great in proportion. Wantonly to sever this more than lifelong compact, and to commence new relations of the same kind, while the other party to the compact is yet alive, is stigmatised in one word as "adultery[u]." Nay, as though to deepen and intensify the sense of the sacredness of marriage, even re-marriage, in any case whatever, is rather discouraged than otherwise[v]. On every side the wedded life is fenced about, like holy ground, from rash precipitancy, from fickleness and instability of purpose, from the intrusion of all low associations. Wedded love is to be undivided, undistracted, concentrating itself—

"To love one only and to cleave to her[w];"

not losing itself aimlessly; the large-hearted, generous love which—

"Alters not when it alteration finds,
Nor bends with the remover to remove[x]."

Can this tender reverence for marriage be paralleled outside Christianity, even in the strictest days of the Roman Republic, even in the purest traditions of the Hebrew law? And, if we look for the vital principle of it, we find it here, as always in Christianity, to be that love of Christ which draws Him and His people together inseparably for ever. The

[u] St. Matt. v. 32; xix. 9; Rom. vii. 3.   [v] 1 Cor. vii. 10, 11.
[w] Tennyson, *Dedicat. Pref. to Idylls of the King*.   [x] Shakesp., *Sonnets*.

mutual trust and joy of the wedded life are an emblem of the soul's communion with its Redeemer, nay, rather an expression and a realization of the same feeling. The Church is "a chaste virgin espoused to one husband;"—the Bride, "adorned for her Lord," waiting on earth with eager fidelity for his long-promised return. He is the Bridegroom, absent and far away, yet ever watching over His Church, as a man cherishes "the wife of his bosom[y]." Can we wonder if, with so high, so pure an ideal before their eyes of what wedded love may be, Christians, with all their controversial differences, with all their inconsistencies in practice, have nevertheless consented in regarding the holiness of marriage as a distinctive and fundamental tenet [z]?

Indeed, the position which woman holds in Christianity is absolutely unique. Bound to a loving obedience, yet not the slave, the drudge of her lord;

---

[y] St. Matthew ix. 15; St. John iii. 29; 2 Cor. xi. 2; Rev. xix. 7, xxi. 2, 9, xxii. 17.

[z] And yet we are told, "No Apostle seems to have been aware, nor does Jesus teach, that love ennobles and spiritualizes," (*F. W. Newman's Defective Morality of the New Testament*, p. 24,) and that "defilement with women in the Apocalypse" means "marriage," (*Ib.*, p. 27.) The same writer (*Ib.*, p. 28) adds, in the face of 1 Cor. vii. 1—17, "the reasons which Paul gives for marriage are not moral." It is important to discriminate in this passage between the general principle which the Apostle lays down of the lawfulness of marriage, and his personal preference for the unmarried life under existing circumstances, (cf. vv. 2, 7).

The compatibility of marriage with perfect devotion to God is beautifully expressed by Keble, *Christian Year*, Wednesday before Easter:—

"And there are souls," &c.

not the toy of his fleeting passion, but his "yokefellow" in all the joys and sorrows of life; his helpmate in all those gentler avocations, for which the softness and delicacy of her temperament fit her, without arrogating to herself his proper functions; endeared to him by the very weakness which looks up to his protecting care, and yet all the time wellnigh worshipped by him for the graces of which her outward form is the interpreter,—this is Christian womanhood. Pagan and Christian art, each in its way, have given us types of female beauty, types which will live for ever, in the voluptuous charms of the Paphian queen rising from the waves, in the more spiritual loveliness of sweet and saintly Madonnas. As we stand and gaze at these masterpieces of the chisel and of the brush, can we doubt which of these two ideals of womanhood is the higher; in other words, which of the two awakens the more unselfish love?

Yes! this tender reverence for women is no mere product of culture and civilization, for it was unknown to Greece and Rome in the zenith of their refinement; it is no heritage of race, for the Freya of Northern Europe is the Aphrodite of Greece; it does not date its existence[a] from the days of tilt and tournament, though chivalry and feudality may have helped to develope and deepen it; it is the reflexion on earth of that self-devoting love which

---

[a] Guizot attributes it to the isolation of the feudal castle (*Histoire de la Civilisation en Europe*, pp. 106, 107). But the isolation of the harem produces a directly opposite effect.

brought the Son of God down from heaven; it is an echo of those accents which, on the hills of Galilee and in the streets of Jerusalem, ever drew to the Saviour's side those who needed His love the most.

> "Through all channels, good and evil,
>   Love from its pure source enticed,
> Finds its own eternal level
>   In the charity of Christ.
> Ye who hear, behold the river
>   Whence it cometh, whither goes—
> Glory be to God the Giver,
>   From whose throne the river flows;
> Flows and streams through all creation,
>   Counter-charm of every curse,
> Love—the waters of salvation
>   Flowing through the universe [b]."

[b] Tannhaüser.

LECTURE IV.

Christianity and Ambition.

2 CORINTHIANS viii. 9.

"*Though He was rich, yet for your sakes He became poor, that ye through His poverty might be rich.*"

NEXT in order to the appetites of the body come the desires of personal aggrandisement; that is, of wealth and power, or rather, in one word, of power. For money is only a means to an end; valuable from a selfish point of view, either for the comfort and luxury which it can purchase, or for the larger importance and wider influence which it symbolises, and for the acquisition of which it is one of the things most needful. The miser gloating over his useless hoards for their own sake, ever amassing without any ulterior purpose, is simply a monstrous anomaly, too monstrous to be worth noticing. Now, so far as wealth ministers to the pleasures of sense, it need not occupy us now, since these have been considered in a previous lecture. It remains only to regard wealth as one among the incentives to those forms of self-love which we may class together under the name of covetousness or ambition. The virtues especially called into play by these desires are obviously truth, honesty, justice, frugality, industry, liberality. The correlative vices, whether of excess or defect, there is no need to specify.

That Christianity has promoted open-handedness in giving, while, by proposing beneficence as the end and object of saving, it rescues frugality from its innate tendency to become parsimony, is not questioned, and cannot be. Indeed, if we are to believe the opponents of Christianity, a Quixotic propensity to excessive almsgiving is one of its worst blemishes. It may be worth while to dwell some little time on this point.

"No prominence is given in Christianity to justice;" so writes one of the ablest of those who have impugned Christianity "as a virtue of prime importance[a]." The same writer hails the dawn of some "nobler religion, which will establish a more general good-will through justice than endless talk about love will ever produce[b]." But the antithesis is unpractical and unreal; unless we are to take justice in the hardest and narrowest conception possible, as weighing men's rights and wrongs, like the Jew's pound of flesh, to the fraction of an ounce, and rigidly disallowing any the most infinitesimal variation from its prescript. But there is a higher, truer justice than this. The man whom the old philosophy terms ἐπιεικής is far above the ἀκριβοδίκαιος[c]. Equity, in place of this dry conformity to the letter, which may be, and often is, a gross injustice in spirit, takes into account all circumstances which may intensify or extenuate the praise or the blame in each particular instance. With-

---

[a] F. W. Newman, *On the Defective Morality of the New Testament*, p. 19. [b] Ibid., p. 33.

[c] Arist., *Nicom. Eth.*, v. 10, 8.

out these considerations to temper judgment, true justice is not, cannot be. And this considerateness depends for its very being on love. For without sympathy a true understanding is impossible of rights and wrongs, of merit and demerit. The absence of sympathy, the presence of antipathy, prejudice the appreciation of persons and things. "The only way," it has been said, "of knowing human nature is to love it; and it can only be won at this price [d]." Therefore, to oppose Justice to Love, as though either could exist independently of the other, is unreasonable.

But is it true in any sense, that "no prominence is given in Christianity to justice as a virtue of prime importance?" It would be nearer the truth to say, that the idea of justice pervades the Gospel from beginning to end. When the approach of Christ is heralded by His forerunner, it is thus: "He shall turn the disobedient to the wisdom of the just [e]." When the final day of reckoning is foretold, that day is to sever the "just from the unjust [f]." But it would be superfluous to string together the many passages in the New Testament where justice is used as a synonym for holiness, in order to shew that the virtue which is the basis on which the superstructure of all other virtues must be reared, and on which society depends for its coherence, is not slurred over by Christianity, or thrust into the background as if it were not "of prime importance." Nay, to

[d] Ozanam.   [e] St. Luke i. 17.   [f] St. Matt. xiii. 49.

be honourable—and I need not remind you either that the Greek word rendered "honest" in our version would rather be in our modern English "honourable," or that a finer sense of honour has been a specialty of Christianity—implies more than to be just; and honour includes strict justice as the greater includes the less[g]. But we must pass on to meet other allegations.

Christianity is accused of fostering a "profuse charity," and by consequence a habit of "mendicancy"[h]; and with a singular misapprehension of the relative proportion of things, the writer already quoted speaks of "communion of goods as the only visible religious peculiarity of the early Christian Church[i];" as if Stephen had been stoned, Peter imprisoned, Paul mobbed, "the brethren" persecuted from city to city, as being Communists.

This imputation of encouraging a mischievous indiscriminate almsgiving, if substantiated, would argue a serious fault in evangelic morality. For the *reductio ad absurdum* is obvious. "To command *all* men to sell their property is to command an absurdity; for if all tried to obey, there would be no buyers[j]."

---

[g] As the motive in Christianity is more unselfish, so the sense of honour is more exquisite. Stoicism, by the mouth of the Stoic Emperor, teaches, "Lie not, even in things indifferent, *for it weakens the understanding.*"—G. Long, *M. Aurelius Antoninus*, p. 62. Christianity teaches, "Lie not one to another, *for ye are brethren in the Lord.*"

[h] F. W. Newman, *On the Defective Morality of the Gospel*, p. 10.

[i] F. W. Newman, *Against Hero-making in Religion*, p. 9.   [j] Ibid.

It might be added, the precept, "Give to him that asketh [k]," if it meant incessant and indiscriminate almsgiving, would be similarly its own refutation. But the very fact that words like these cannot be taken in their naked literalness, implies of necessity that some qualification is understood by a mental ellipsis to complete the sentence. The allegation loses its force, nay, falls to the ground utterly, if for disjointed texts we substitute the whole tenor and drift of the Gospel's teaching; if, as in fairness we are bound to do, we see in its words not so many stereotyped rules, but organic principles, addressed, indeed, primarily, with a special intention to a special occasion, and yet instinct with a germinative life, unfolding itself continually to ever-varying requirements.

Let us take the instances in question. The charge of Communism against the Church at Jerusalem is soon disposed of. The very narrative on which it rests, plainly shews that the husband and wife, whose names have become a byword for the pretence of sanctity without the reality, had full right to keep their property from the common fund, if they were so minded. "Whilst it remained, was it not thine own?" the Apostle asks; and even "after it was sold, was it not in thine own power[1]?" Clearly, when we read how "the multitude of them which believed were of one heart and of one soul; neither said any of them, that aught which he possessed was his own,

---

[k] St. Matt. v. 42.   [1] Acts v. 4.

for they had all things common[m]," we are to understand no confiscation of property, but that closeness and tenderness of sympathy which bound rich and poor together in one, till the corrosive influences of the world had sundered this fellowship of "the brethren in the Lord."

Or take the case,—for it is a crucial one,—of the Rich Young Man, to whom were addressed those memorable words, which provoke the especial indignation of the able sceptic already quoted, "If thou wilt be perfect, go thy way, sell all thou hast, and give to the poor[n]." These are the words which he stigmatises as "a fierce threat," "a crushing, arbitrary command[o];" words which certainly fall on the ear with something of harshness and austerity, and which, if they stood alone, might seem to extort from the followers of Christ a precipitate renunciation of all their worldly possessions. These are the words which sounded as a call from heaven to Antony, as he worshipped in a church of Alexandria, and longed for some heroic act of self-abnegation. These are the words which fired the son of a merchant at Assisi to forsake "his own people and his father's house," for a brotherhood of barefooted friars. And it has been with a view to escape from what to a cooler judgment seems a suicidal infatuation, and would be, if it ever could become general, simply annihilative of our social life with its manifold privileges and responsibilities, that a distinction, delusive and

[m] Acts iv. 32. [n] St. Matt. xix. 21. [o] F. W. Newman, *Against Hero-making in Religion*, p. 18.

impracticable, has been invented by casuists between "counsels of perfection" for saints, and a lower standard of obedience for ordinary Christians. But the main solution of the difficulty is to be found in that trite old caution, never out of date, necessary alike for those to whom Christianity is an offence, and for those among Christians who exaggerate some favourite dogma or precept out of proportion,—that one side of the truth must always be complemented by the other; a caution necessary most of all in regard to a teaching so essentially *suggestive* as that of the Gospel, and without which the truth itself becomes a lie.

For here surely, and here alone, is the key to this and other similar injunctions of Christ; first, to mark the symptoms of the moral state of the person addressed [p]; for the great Physician adapts his remedies to each one's needs, and his glance, like the touch of Ithuriel's spear, detects self-deceit in its disguise: next, from this moral diagnosis in the mind of Christ to discover the intention which makes the precept of universal application for all similar cases; for human nature repeats itself: and, lastly, to guard the precept from collision with other laws of morality, lest it trespass on ground which they have pre-occupied.

Now even a cursory glance at the narrative shews that the one thing wanted to test the sincerity of this would-be convert, was that he should be forced

---

[p] Compare, for instance, the command to the demoniac (St. Mark v. 19), and to the leper (St. Matt. viii. 4).

to ask himself that question, which one way or another all must ask of their own souls, and answer, "Am I willing to part with what I love best in the world for the truth's sake?" It is easy to play the hero when self has nothing at stake. The latent selfishness betrays itself in the words, "Good Master, what good thing shall I do, that I may have eternal life[q]?" It meets its indirect reproof in the demurrer of Christ to be called "good" by one whose notion of goodness was dwarfed by selfishness. To have kept this or that commandment might be, to one naturally so disposed, little more than a supine acquiescence. The touchstone of real unselfishness was to consent to shatter his idol. This he would not; and thus self-convicted of unreality he went away, we are told, sorrowing. Surely the gist of all these precepts of self-abnegation, which only the wildest fanaticism can take as they stand—cut off the right hand, pluck out thine eye, submit unresistingly to every insult, to every outrage, fling thine alms broadcast to every mendicant, provide nothing, take no thought for the morrow—is briefly this: Whatever usurps the place in thine heart where love should reign, must be dethroned—be the pang what it may—and cast away.

But a charge, diametrically opposed to those of reckless improvidence and of lavish almsgiving, comes from the same quarter. The teaching of Christ is accused, almost in the same breath, of fostering a temper improvident and yet mercenary. The combination is startling. In the very instance just cited,

[q] St. Matt. xix. 16.

in His interview with the rich young man, our Lord is represented as "dealing in low motives and thoughts of reward—promises of power—salvation by works — investment of money for returns beyond the grave—prudential adoption of virtue which may soften judgment, win promotion, deliver from prospective judgment and hell-fire[r]." It is asked, "Does such a teacher build from within by implanting love —does he act upon love at all, or on a selfish ambition?" And it is added with an indiscriminating generalisation, "In the mind of Jesus all actions seem to stand in the closest relation to the thoughts of punishment and reward on a great future day." "I seek in vain," says the writer, "for anything to implant in the heart a sense of freedom, to excite willing service, gratitude, tranquil love, careless of other reward than love." These are caustic and incisive words. Are they true?

Now without quoting, appealing to, that personal devotion to a personal Saviour which is a special characteristic of St. Paul's writings[s], and which has its practical embodiment in his sublime description of charity, let us confine ourselves at present to the teaching of Christ Himself. Let it be freely granted, as it must be in fairness, that our Lord very frequently enforces His moral dictates through the hope of reward, and through the fear of punish-

---

[r] F. W. Newman, *Against Hero-making in Religion*, p. 19.

[s] Professor Newman arbitrarily excludes all reference to St. Paul on this point, allowing that the Apostle's "precepts are, concerning property, in full agreement with those of Greek and Roman sages," but contending that they "are widely different from those of Jesus."—*On the Defective Morality of the New Testament*, p. 11.

ment hereafter. But what then? These hopes and fears are not the essence of the motive, but auxiliary and subsidiary to it; useful in stemming the force of temptations well-nigh irresistible, as the swimmer seizes a drifting spar in his struggle with the waves. Those whom the Saviour was primarily addressing were not men with their minds illuminated by the flash of an instantaneous revelation. They were to have a slow and gradual discipline before becoming in His Name the teachers of the world. With their inveterate prepossessions about a Messiah who should inaugurate a reign of mundane felicity, with their minds steeped in the Mosaic traditions of temporal rewards and punishments, they needed, like children, all possible support from without for the nascent efforts of the soul within. No parent or teacher would act otherwise with a child, unless in defiance of the laws of our nature. These promises and threats are as a framework round a tender plant, a defence against the blast, till its inner life is matured: but all the time the inner life is nourished, not by these adventitious appliances, but by deep and secret contact with the parent earth.

Nor may it be forgotten that these promises and threatenings are at most only one aspect of the teaching of Christ. "In the world ye shall have tribulation[t]," for your Leader is the homeless one, "a man of sorrows and acquainted with grief." Forbear dreams of your own greatness, "for He is meek and lowly of heart[u]." "Take up thy cross[x]" and bear it unflinchingly, for thy Lord must die on it the death

[t] St. John xvi. 33.   [u] St. Matt. xi. 29.   [x] Ibid. xvi. 24.

of a slave and a malefactor. "Can ye drink of My cup of sorrow? Can ye be baptised with My baptism of blood?" Christ[y] demands of those whose hearts are intent on sharing His glory, who are in thought anticipating the day when they "shall sit on thrones, judging the twelve tribes of Israel[z]." But I need not multiply these presageful warnings of the self-renunciation required from those who would be followers of Jesus. The joys foretold are far away, the sufferings are imminent. Strange not to see, that to embrace these promises of Christ at such a cost implies a moral conviction that He is indeed the Truth; and that to reiterate these forebodings of what must be endured by His followers, is the part not of one bribing men to His side, but of one who seeks that "willing service" of "gratitude" and of "love" which alone can give the soul "a sense of freedom" from the tyranny of self!

Nor is it to be overlooked that the promises of reward are collective not individualistic. The exaltation, the aggrandisement of the individual are discouraged invariably. When the disciples ask, "What shall we have" because we have addicted ourselves to Thy service? they are answered, under the similitude of the "labourers in the vineyard[a]," that they are to work for love not for pay, with no evil eye to fellow-labourers, with no mutinous murmurs against the Lord of the vineyard. When they dispute among themselves about the preeminence, they are told

[y] St. Matt. xx. 22.   [z] Ibid. xix. 28.
[a] Ibid. xx. 1, *et seq.*

each and all to learn from "a little child[b]" how to be lowest and least in the kingdom of their Lord. Even so honourable a title as that of "Benefactors[c]" they are to disclaim, lest the praise of men should alloy the genuineness of love. The promise of future happiness is not for one or other, singly and separately, the realisation of selfish schemings. The faithful are all to rejoice together, as the reapers in one great harvest-field,—the world. Above all, the reward is Christ Himself. His love is motive and recompense in one. The renunciations are to be for His sake; and the reward is this,—to be near His throne, and to gaze with adoring love on the unveiled radiancy of His Presence. Truly a small inducement, except to those whose hearts have caught from Him that ardour of self-sacrifice which loses itself in love. The selfish might have been allured to the banner of the Cross by promises of inglorious repose, and languid self-gratification; but in the Christian's heaven every faculty of body and soul is consecrated to the willing service of his Lord. "This is life eternal, to know Thee, the only true God, and Jesus Christ whom Thou hast sent."

See what Christianity has done in teaching men "to spend and be spent" for others. Granted, that the fingers of dying men have, ere now, relaxed their grasp of their money-bags from fear and not from love; that the scared conscience has drugged itself by the hope of buying heaven with its ill-gotten hoards; that even into the noblest breast will intrude at times

[b] St. Matt. xviii. 2.   [c] St. Luke xxii. 25.

a selfish thought of recompense; still, all this fails utterly to account for the innumerable enterprises which Christianity has initiated, to assuage and alleviate the woes which it cannot prevent, as it tracks the devastating course of sin and sorrow through the world. Christianity proclaims a communism not of constraint, but of will. Property is a sacred thing, it tells us [d]; because it is to be employed for the good of others. The poor must be frugal and industrious, it teaches; that they too may have to give to the more needy than themselves [e]. If ever, as some predict, Christianity could become a thing of the past, its hospitals, its orphanages, its schools [f] would remain the trophies of its bloodless victories over the greediness of Mammon. No cautious balancing of future loss and gain could have called these things into being. It is what the great Apostle felt when he owned himself "debtor [g]" to all men for His Saviour's sake; in one word, it is gratitude. It is unselfish gratitude to One, who, though He was rich, yet for our sakes made Himself poor; who, being Lord of all things, stooped for us to the manger at Bethlehem and the Cross on Calvary; who bared Himself of the glory which He had from the beginning, to wrap forlorn and destitute humanity in its celestial folds.

[d] e.g. Rom. vii. 7.   [e] Eph. iv. 28.   [f] Cf. Lecky, *History of European Morals*, ii. 34.   [g] Rom. i. 14.

LECTURE V.

Christianity and Self-dependence.

ROMANS xiv. 7.

"*None of us liveth to himself, and no man dieth to himself.*"

AS we ascend in thought from the importunities of sense and the solicitations of ambition, to those emotions in our nature which are more independent of external things, we breathe a finer atmosphere, the view widens below our feet, and the path of Christian morality diverges more determinately than ever from that of the morality which is not Christian. Hitherto the difference has been, for the most part, either in the motive which animates the strivings of humanity after perfection, or in the degree of success which these strivings obtain. But here we have in Christianity a diametrically opposite ideal of perfection set before us for imitation. Humility, in the true sense of the word, is as distinctively a Christian virtue, as self-dependence, the crown and culmination of non-Christian morality, is in the Gospel of Christ a weakness and a vice.

For self-dependence is pride; and pride, rather than ambition, deserves to be called

"The last infirmity of noble minds."

When the lower desires have been reduced to submission, when the soul can look down from its philosophic watch-tower on cravings for wealth or power, then, and because of these triumphs which it has achieved, it is in danger of pride. And pride is not only the subtlest form of self-love, but the worst; for it is the perversion of the noblest faculties to a most ignoble end, the deification of self; it is cruelty without the excuse of passion. The foe, repulsed from the outposts, works surreptitiously his insidious way into the citadel itself; and the fortress falls at the very moment when its defenders dream themselves most secure from peril.

Genuine humility, as the experience of all time shews, is the rarest, because the hardest of virtues; the hardest, because it involves the most absolute uprooting of self from the system. No virtue has so many or so plausible counterfeits. The self-depreciation which courts praise is not humility; the indifference to praise, which is contempt for others, is not humility; nay, the humility which secretly and half-unconsciously lauds itself in and for the very act of self-condemnation is but a spurious humility, like the cynic's pride thinly veiled under his ostentatious tatters. Nowhere is the involuntary homage which vice pays to virtue more strikingly exemplified than by these semblances of humility, which pass current in the world, so as almost to defy detection.

Now, of all the characteristics of the Son of Man, humility is the most remarkable. To those who see in Him the Son of God incarnate, no words can express the depth of His self-imposed humiliation.

Even those to whom He is only a Teacher among teachers, one among many leaders of the multitude, cannot but admire His divine calmness under obloquy and insult, as well as amid the Hosannas of the crowd; the calmness not of apathy, but of a nature exquisitely tender in its sympathies[a]. Even they will admit, that, notwithstanding many inconsistencies in practice, this "meekness and lowliness" of spirit have been an especial badge of those who take "His yoke upon[b]" their shoulders, and learn of Him that self must be as nothing, and love as everything in the hearts of His disciples.

Self-reliance is in other systems the aim and object of all the upward soarings of the soul. For, if the health of his soul is the first thing for a man to consider; if virtue is health, vice disease[c]; then, though beneficence to others may be a duty, as subserving self-culture, still, the primary law being self-preservation, the summit of moral perfection is to rise above every feeling which can obstruct this work of self-improvement, which can mar the symmetry, the harmony, the autarchy, the entelechy of the soul. There must, indeed, be no outward manifestation of this inward consciousness of strength. That would be arrogance; and arrogance would be a flaw in the circle of self-dependence, as betokening a recognition, however contemptuous, of other existences than our own[d]. But the consciousness itself must be there.

Take, for instance, that system of philosophy, of

---

[a] e.g. St. John xi. 35.   [b] St. Matt. xi. 29.   [c] Grote's *Plato*, iii. 131.   [d] M. Antonin., *Meditat.*, ii. 17.

which it has been said by a great Christian thinker that it comes "nearest to Christianity[e];" which, indeed, like Christianity, lifts the soul above the trivial hopes and fears of the world of sense, and, like Christianity, makes virtue independent of success and failure, of good fortune or bad; although its hardness, its ἀναισθησία, contrasts strongly with a teaching which, instead of ruthlessly extirpating the affections[f], trains them tenderly round whatever it can find worthiest in earth or heaven;—take Stoicism. "Be like the Olympian Jove of Phidias," the Stoic writes, "in an unclouded confidence and strength[g]." In other words, "Be self-contained, self-centred, self-orbed. So will you be able to look down with pity, if not with contempt, on the errors and delusions of the multitude." We have not so learned from our Master. In strange contrast to this self-conscious, self-satisfied intellectuality, Christ teaches His disciples to be as children, teachable and lowly, for their strength is to be perfected in weakness[h], and out of weakness they are to be made strong[i]. His sternest denunciations are not against sins of passion, but against a hard and scornful self-righteousness. The prayer which He best approves is, "God be merciful to me a sinner[k]." The verdict of acquittal, of commendation at the last, is for those who are least aware of their own merits; who ask in unfeigned astonish-

---

[e] S. T. Coleridge, *Aids to Reflection*, p. 62.   [f] Cf. Tacit., *Agric.*, 30.   [g] Arrian., ii. 8, quoted by Lecky, *Hist. of European Morals*, i. p. 161.   [h] 2 Cor. xii. 9.   [i] Heb. xi. 34.   [k] St. Luke xviii. 13.

ment of their Judge, "When have we done aught for Thee¹?" Fearless of the sneers of supercilious Pharisees, Christ sits at meat, by a preference to them hopelessly unintelligible, under the roof of "publicans and sinners ᵐ;" and singles out for a special blessing the outcast whose only plea is this, that she has "loved much ⁿ."

Stoicism and Christianity alike teach, that the life of man consists not in those external appliances which to so many seem to constitute the idea of living, but in the perfection of the soul; that this alone is life. Both alike enjoin strictest self-examination °. But the practical character of this self-examination, in the one case and the other, differs as widely as the dialectical promptings of the Demon of Socrates from the persuasive influences of the Holy Ghost on the life and will of a Christian ᵖ. In the Pagan philosophy man reviews his own handiwork, effaces a line here, inserts a touch there; studious of the model which he proposes to himself, that he may not have to reproach himself for inadequacy of execution; a severe critic of himself; true to his own conceptions of excellence; and, let it be granted, caring far more to have realized his ideal than for the silly plaudits of the crowd. But, all the time,

---

¹ St. Matt. xxv. 37—39. ᵐ St. Mark ii. 16. ⁿ St. Luke vii. 47.
° e.g. Persius, *Satir.* iv. 21.
ᵖ "The Demon of Socrates was but an intellectual guide, and checked his erring judgment; the Holy Spirit guards the vigils of duty, and succours the disciple's tempted will."—Martineau, *Studies of Christianity*, p. 307.

he begins and ends his task in himself. In Christianity the penitent rises from his knees with even the sense of his own unworthiness lost in the sense of God's pardoning love, and in sympathetic tenderness for his fellow-sinners. Marcus Aurelius has been fitly styled "the purest, gentlest spirit of the Pagan world [q];" his writings, "the highest ethical product of the heathen mind [r]." In words which sound like an echo from Calvary, he says, "Love those who have offended you, for they do it ignorantly," they "know not what they do [s]." But mark the undercurrent of thought and feeling. I am not unfair, I trust, to this noble Roman if I read it thus: "It is beneath philosophy to waste a thought on beings so unworthy; hatred is a perturbation of that tranquillity of spirit which we aim at; life is too short; the work of self-improvement too momentous [t]." But Christian forgiveness is rather thus: "How can I refuse to forgive others, I who am myself so greatly forgiven? How can I but prefer others in honour, I who know so well my own deficiencies?" "For none of us liveth to himself, and no man dieth to himself: whether we live or die, we are the Lord's." In brief, Stoicism is a deification of man for himself [u]; Christianity is a deification of man for his God and for his fellows.

[q] Lecky, *History of European Morals*, i. 219.   [r] J. S. Mill, *On Liberty*, p. 15.   [s] *Meditat.*, vii. 22.   [t] *Medit.*, vii. 26; ii. 17; xi. 18.

[u] What has been said of Buddhism, "It is a barren waste of intellectual perfection," (M. Müller, *Buddhism*, p. 19,) may not unfairly be said of Stoicism.

These intense yearnings of sympathy flow directly and flow exclusively from the Cross on Calvary. For there we see, not, as some have represented it, a mere substitution on the sacrificial altar of one victim for another, not the mere intervention of a stranger paying down a sum for those who cannot pay, but heaven condescending to identify itself with the sins and sorrows of earth; the divine nature attuned by love to perfect unison with the heart-throbbings of humanity. "Greater love hath no man than this, that a man lay down his life for his friends." And the Christian's faith or love, call it as you will, involves a responsive unification of himself with the lowest and weakest of his brethren. This it is which sent forth Saul of Tarsus, Boniface, Xavier, Schwartz, Patteson, to lay down their lives for those who, aliens and outcasts in the world's estimation, were brought near to them by the very extremity of their need. "No Jew, Greek, Roman, Brahman," it has been said by one especially competent to speak on the subject, "ever thought of converting people to his own national form of belief[x]." Even in Buddhism can we find an instance of so entire a sympathy with the wretched, as that which has induced Christian missionaries to devote themselves to a forlorn and lifelong exile on an island peopled only by lepers[y], in the spirit of Him who laid His healing hand on the miserable victims of this loathsome malady, who on the eve of His own agony stooped down and washed His own betrayer's feet, who shrank not from the polluted touch of the woman

---

[x] M. Müller, *Buddhism*, p. 22.   [y] In the Greek Archipelago.

who had been a grievous sinner? Others may teach, that it is politic and right to leave the stricken deer to pine and die alone, while the herd makes for fresh pastures. Not so the Gospel of Christ. There, even unworthiness has a claim on those who feel their own unworthiness in the presence of their Saviour.

To the Stoic, even to one like Marcus Aurelius, pain, bodily or mental, is simply a thing to be endured as best may be. Dimly and uncertainly through the mysterious darkness of sorrow he sees that pain is a teacher, and the only teacher, for those who refuse to learn otherwise. But to him it comes only as a disagreeable consequence of having infringed a law stronger than himself,—of having blindly come into collision with nature and had the worst of it. He has foolishly allowed himself to be caught and entangled in the resistless, relentless mechanism of the universe, and must pay the penalty; he must extricate himself from his dilemma, if he can, with a firm resolve to be more wary lest he jeopardise himself again; if not, he may as well cut short his troubles summarily and for ever, by making a speedy exit from a struggle in which pride forbids him to confess himself beaten. It is useless, he argues, to contend against what must be; Fate is inexorable; and so, with sullen and defiant acquiescence, he accepts what he cannot avoid[z]. But the Christian is taught, that suffering is not merely penal, but remedial for the sufferer; that it is the "loving correction" which a Father inflicts reluctantly; the sharp but momentary pang which a wise and tender healer, probing and cauter-

[z] M. Antonin., *Meditat.*, xi. 18, ii. 17.

ising the wound, knows must be submitted to; that patience can only thus have "her perfect work [a];" that the Son of God Himself, in His life on earth, had to "learn obedience by the things which He suffered," and that there is no other school for His followers; that the gold must be purged of its dross in the fire; that the spikenard must be bruised and broken, or it will not yield the sweetness which is in it; in short, that pride, the last stronghold of self in the heart, must be levelled with the ground, for love to be all in all.

Nor is there, as some say, anything mean or pusillanimous in Christian humility. Because the Gospel commends the "poor in spirit [b];" because it preaches, "Resist not evil [c];" because it seems to a hasty glance to inculcate a tame and abject submission to extortion and oppression [d], we are told that Christianity is wanting in self-assertion. But these precepts, as was observed in a previous lecture, if they are to have any meaning at all, must be understood with those qualifications which are suggested by comparing them with other passages, by supplying the omissions, incidental to speech always, and too obvious to need specifying; above all, by having regard to the mental and moral capacity of those on whose ears they fell in the first instance. "The letter killeth, but the spirit giveth life [e]." We must bear in mind, that these precepts of submission were spoken to men of a nation more stubbornly tena-

[a] St. James i. 4.   [b] St. Matt. v. 3.   [c] Ibid. v. 39.
[d] Ibid. v.   [e] 2 Cor. iii. 6.

cious, perhaps, than any other of its self-assertion; to men who had been taught from childhood that merciless retaliation is a sacred duty, that "eye for eye," "tooth for tooth [f]," is not merely excusable, but right. We must bear in mind that an utter disruption of law and order would ensue, if the words were taken literally, and without context. We must bear in mind that the same Teacher who says, "Resist not evil [g]," tells His "little flock [h]," when left in the world like "sheep among wolves [i]," and "without a shepherd," to "fear not," even though dragged "before synagogues, and magistrates, and powers [k];" but to confess their Master boldly before men, without a thought of the shame, or of the peril;—that He, who pleaded so tenderly for His disciples, "Let these go their way," Himself confronted His foes with the intrepid declaration, "I am He;"—that He trod the winepress alone, and drained the cup of agony to the dregs, not, indeed, without shrinking, but with an unwavering purpose, to save others at any cost to Himself. Clearly the gist of these precepts of submission is this,—to exorcise from the heart the spirit of self-assertion, so far as it conflicts with duty; to foster and encourage self-assertion, so far as it stands forward as the champion of others, "fighting the good fight [l]" under the banner of Love. Paradoxical as it may sound, the truest courage, nay, the only true courage, is, like real magnanimity, inseparable from humility. For true

[f] St. Matt. v. 38. [g] Ibid. v. 39. [h] St. Luke xii. 32.
[i] St. Matt. x. 16. [k] St. Luke xii. 11. [l] 2 Tim. iv. 7.

courage differs from rashness, from empty boastfulness in this, that it implies a true estimate of the dangers to be faced, and of a man's own ability to face them; it measures the hazard, and counts the cost, and yet is content to abide the issue. The martyrs of Antioch or of Lyons, lavish of their own lives, refusing to avail themselves of any subterfuge, however venial, from the dungeon, the stake, the lions of the amphitheatre, were they timid, vacillating, irresolute? Was it a pusillanimous spirit, which, not satisfied with the persistent profession of its own faith, dared even to affront, in its aggressive zeal for Christ, the massive organization, the pitiless inflexibility of the Roman Empire? The martyrs and confessors of Christianity are rather liable to the charge of provoking persecution and of courting death, than of cowardice.

Nor is there anything mawkish or feebly sentimental in Christian humility. With all its compassion for the sinner, it never condones the sin. The Antinomianism which "sins that grace may abound[m]," which almost glories in wrong-doing, in its eagerness to magnify the Atonement, is a caricature of the Gospel of Christ, intolerable to the reason and conscience of men. What was said of the great mediæval poet of Christendom,—

"He loved well, because he hated,"

is essentially true of Christianity. Uncompromising hatred of evil is an integral part of Christian love.

[m] Rom. vi. 1.

There is no place in Christianity for the lukewarm zeal of Laodicea. "He that is not with Me," Christ has said, "is against Me;" "he that gathereth not with Me, scattereth ⁿ." The same voice, which so often breathed pardon and peace on penitents, whom Pharisaic scorn would have spurned from His feet, denounced, in tones wherein even pity is well-nigh drowned in sternness of reproof, the sin which would not own itself sinful, which in its pride hardened itself even against love.

Nor, lastly, can Christian humility be fairly accused—whatever pretext for the accusation may have been given by fanatical distortions of Christianity—of a morbid self-depreciation, of a morbid exaggeration of its own wretchedness. The Christian may not feel contempt,—even for himself. While prostrating himself in his self-abasement before the glorious ideal which he fails to realise, while "abhorring himself in dust and ashes," he still cannot forget that human nature was created in the likeness of the divine; that this image of God on the soul, tarnished and defaced by sin, was restored by the incarnation of divinity; that it is continually renewed by the sweet influences of the Holy Spirit. "Self-reverence," as well as "self-distrust," is part of "self-knowledge" in a Christian º.

> "True dignity abides with him alone,
> Who, in the silent hour of inward thought,
> Can still suspect and still revere himself
> In lowliness of heart ᵖ."

ⁿ St. Matt. xii. 30. º "Self-reverence, self-knowledge, self-distrust."—*Tennyson, Œnone.* ᵖ Wordsworth.

To the Stoic or the Buddhist, baffled and foiled in his struggles to break loose from the thraldom of evil, only one escape is left,—self-annihilation. To the Christian, failure and disappointment, even in the pursuit of holiness, are an incentive to new exertions. His hopefulness can never die, for the mainspring of hope is without, not within the soul. To him despair is an impossibility, for, in the "darkness that may be felt," the soul casts itself the more undoubtingly on the love which never changes. For

> ".... all through life I see a Cross,
> Where sons of God yield up their breath;
> There is no gain except by loss;
> There is no life except in death;
> Nor glory, but in bearing shame;
> Nor justice, but in taking blame;
> And that eternal Passion saith,
> 'Be emptied of glory, and right, and name¹!'"

¹ *Olric Grange.* (Madehouse, Glasgow.)

LECTURE VI.

The Universality of Christian Morality.

GENESIS xxiii. 18.

"*In Him shall all nations of the earth be blessed.*"

WE have completed—if such a word is pardonable of what is, I am well aware, so incomplete—our survey of the emotions, and of the treatment which they receive from Christianity and from other systems. Let us ascend in thought higher still. Let us contemplate, as from the mountain's summit, one of the most important characteristics of Christian morals, their universality.

No one can be conversant with the poetry and philosophy which exhibit civilization before the Christian era in its highest form, without observing how incommensurate they are with the life of man as a whole. So far as life is sunny, joyous, prosperous, they express it well; with less indeed of reserve and of qualification, with a more thorough abandonment to it for the moment than is possible for one whose religion teaches him to grieve for others, if not for himself. But life is not all sunshine. None are exempt—it is a truism to say it—from pain; to many, if not to most, painful experiences preponderate over pleasurable; while over our brightest moments death, ever drawing near, casts its dark shadow before. And here Pagan philosophy fails us in our need. Mark the undercurrent of sadness, nay, of utter hopelessness, which ever and anon forces itself to the surface, as we listen to the festive lyrics of Horace, crowned with roses, and with the wine-cup in his hand. See how Stoicism, in its despairing effort to assert its indifference to evils which it can neither remedy nor explain, has only one word of comfort for its votary; that he fold himself in his toga and die [a]. The philosophies of Zeno, or of Epicurus, stand dumb before the Sphinx of man's destiny with its insoluble enigma; they would fain escape, if they could, from the stony gaze of those pitiless eyes. But Christianity faces every aspect of our existence, sunlit or under the cloud. It is no privilege of the rich, the learned, the prosperous. It knows "how to be abased and how to abound [b]." It bids its disciples "rejoice with those that do rejoice," as well as "weep with those that weep [c]." And if joy is impossible for souls beset, beaten down, all but crushed under their woes, it whispers of a "peace which passes understanding [d]."

See, again, how each race of mankind contributes its portion to the common fund of Christian morality, and derives thence in return something which it desiderates. The Hebrew brings his stubborn tenacity of conscience and conviction, and in the crucible of the Gospel what was hard and unsympathetic glows with the ardour of a world-wide diffusiveness. The

[a] See Note C. [b] Phil. iv. 12.
[c] Rom. xii. 15. [d] Phil. iv. 7.

Greek brings his readiness of invention in art and science, and what was sensuous, material, selfish, is transfigured with a glory not of earth. The Roman brings his soldier-like obedience to order, the Teuton his rugged loyalty to hearth and home, and both alike learn that an uncompromising sense of duty is strengthened, not weakened, by tenderness of feeling. Like the gate of a mediæval monastery, Christianity opens itself to all comers; welcomes all to its shelter; receives from each his peculiar inheritance of truth; imparts to each that which was wanting to complete it, and fuses the scattered fragments into a whole.

Or mark the elasticity of Christianity in adapting itself to various forms of government. True: in our own experience, as elsewhere, the Church of Christ has not always been proof against the temptation of identifying itself with a political party. True: in the past history of this country, as elsewhere, the Church has, ere now, clung with unreasoning fidelity to a dynasty that has ceased to represent the nation. Still, if we review the course of ecclesiastical history from first to last, it is clear that the Gospel is no hothouse exotic, only kept alive by artificial appliances, but a hardy plant, that can thrive, if need be, on the bleak mountain side. The Gospel precept of obedience to those who are in authority, applies alike to the subjects of a despotic empire, of a constitutional monarchy, of a democracy where all are on a level. When the French republican of the last century called the Founder of Christianity "le bon sansculotte," and when the Jacobite adherent of the exiled

Stuarts appealed to his creed as teaching him to "honour the king," they were unconsciously combining their testimony to the breadth and elasticity of Christian politics. When the words "Unity, Indivisibility, Brotherhood, or Death," were inscribed over the doors of the houses in Paris in 1790, it was a ghastly parody of the universal fellowship which the Gospel proclaims. For Christianity recognises fully the two great principles, too often forced into an unnatural antagonism, of spontaneity and authority, because it recognises fully the rights of each individual, and the rights of the community at large. On the one hand, it insists unhesitatingly on the priceless value of each man's personality: "What shall a man give in exchange for his soul[e]?" On the other hand, it lays an equal or even greater stress on the reciprocal obligations of society: "For we are members one of another[f]." The obedience which Christianity preaches is no Chinese obedience, no sluggish and unprogressive conformity to routine, for it is tempered and quickened by the ever-present sense of personal freedom, of personal responsibility. The liberty which Christianity proclaims is not anarchy, for though it is "perfect liberty," it is itself a "law[g]."

Mark, again, the absence of minute and vexatious regulations in the oldest records of Christianity. If we look to the life and teaching of Christ, either as pourtrayed in the simple and inartistic narrative of the Gospels, or as thrown into perspective in the

[e] St. Mark viii. 37.   [f] Rom. xii. 5.   [g] St. James i. 25.

Epistles, we find nothing there like the Levitical ordinances, nothing like the grotesque technicalities of the Talmud, or of the Institutes of Menu[h], elaborate enough to occupy a student for a lifetime. The Sermon on the Mount speaks to all, learned and unlearned alike. The rude peasant hears homely rules for the daily ordinary course of his uneventful life. The philosopher, who disdains not to sit at the feet of the meek and lowly Teacher, discerns the great moral principles which hold the world together. All recognise the expression of a something, of which they were half-aware, dimly conscious before; and the heart, like the earth on a morning in spring, feels within itself the stir of a dormant energy. As Bp. Taylor quaintly but beautifully says, the teaching of Christ "enters like rain into a fleece of wool[i]." Even precepts such as these, "to abstain from meat offered to idols[k]," and not to "muzzle the ox that treadeth out the corn[l]," which have been cited as a contradiction of this universality of the Gospel, are no contradiction really. In both cases a great principle underlies an apparently arbitrary enactment. There is the principle of not even seeming to countenance a popular delusion. There is the principle of providing for the temporal wants of those who hold a spiritual office. In both cases the minuteness

[h] "The Institutes of Menu, the Leviticus and Deuteronomy of the Hindus for so many ages, speak of killing . . . . and eating with unwashen hands as crimes of parallel magnitude."—Cobbe, *Darwinism in Morals*, &c., p. 227.
[i] Quoted by Mr. Martineau in his *Studies of Christianity*.
[k] Acts xv. 29.   [l] 1 Cor. ix. 19.

is in the expression, not in the thought; in the illustration, not in the thing illustrated.

The very incompleteness of Christianity as a theory comes from its largeness of conception, from its not being the peculiarity of any age or clime. A French Positivist can elaborate on paper a system to the eye faultless in its symmetry, but experience shews that the practical excellence of a system is not infrequently in an inverse proportion to its excellence in the abstract. "The Christian Scriptures," it has been well said, "are singularly sparing of" (even) "general rules[m]." It has been objected, that the warnings of the Gospel are pointed against sects whose very names have passed away; but in their characteristics the Pharisee and the Sadducee never die; the formalist and the materialist are rife in one age as in another. It has been objected, that the Apostles lived in hourly expectation of their Lord's Second Advent; but to live as servants, always watching for their Lord's return, is a cardinal principle of Christianity. Strip off all that is really local, temporal, personal, from the Christian Scriptures; separate, so far as the human intellect can separate things so closely woven together, the divine and the human elements: in the residuum you find fundamental principles of life, coeval with time, and co-extensive with humanity.

This universality is a characteristic as of Christianity so of its Founder. Sectarian partialities may narrow our conception of Christ Jesus, may exag-

[m] Martineau, *Studies of Christianity*, p. 291.

gerate, may dwarf, may distort this or that feature in His character, but the one-sidedness is not in Him. Nay, to a careless observer the apparent inconsistency almost amounts to paradox. Christ denounces Pharisaism, yet teaches His disciples to obey their Pharisaical rulers. He consorts with Publicans and sinners, and yet teaches that only "the pure in heart shall see God[n]." He rebukes Sabbatarian scruples, and yet conforms sedulously to the very ritual which He is superseding. He proclaims that "God is a Spirit[o]," not confining His presence to the Hill of Sion, or to the rival Mount of the Samaritans, and yet evinces special love and reverence for the Temple, makes it His favourite resort, displays an almost unique severity of castigation on its behalf, and even while predicting its downfal and extinction is "consumed[p]" by zeal for its hallowed walls. He teaches "as one having authority[q]," and yet by a course of gentle questionings which evoke intelligence in the dullest or most timid listeners; His parables are like stories for a child, and yet to those who "have ears to hear" are instinct with profoundest mysteries. The catalogue of seeming inconsistencies is well-nigh endless. Unlike His forerunner, the Baptist, austere as a hermit to king, to multitude, to himself, the "Son of Man" (it is our Lord's favourite designation of Himself, and it symbolises the range of His affections) is at home under the roof of Levi the Publican or of Simon the Pharisee; amid the festivities of the mar-

[n] St. Matt. v. 8.   [o] St. John iv. 24.   [p] Ibid. ii. 17.
[q] St. Matt. vii. 29.

riage feast in Cana, or amid the wailings of the chamber of death; has a blessing for the rich man, like Zacchæus, who knows how to use his riches, as for the poor widow dropping her scanty offering into the treasury of God. He is uncompromising with sin, yet tender with the sinner; He walks alone through the crowd, rapt in heavenly musings, yet has an eye for Nathaniel under his fig-tree, and a word of comfort for the nameless sufferer, laying her trembling hand on the hem of His robe; He is unceasing, unresting in doing "His Father's business[r]," crowding almost an infinity of words of wisdom and of works of love into those three short years, yet ever imperturbable in His calmness; He can silence His adversaries with a word, and yet stands without a word when they suborn false witnesses against Him; He is "meek and lowly" with all His majesty of deportment; with all His lowliness He is a King. Truly the heart of the "Son of Man" beats in accord with every pulsation of the hearts of men that is not sinful.

I am not forgetting that this universality of the Gospel is questioned, nay, positively and emphatically denied by some. The able opponent of Christianity, from whom I have had occasion to quote in some previous lectures, flatly rejects the idea as an exploded error. "When people tell me," he writes, "that Jesus first established the brotherhood of man, the equality of races, the nullity of ceremonies; . . . . that He overthrew the narrowness of Judaism; found

[r] St. Luke ii. 49.

a national but left an universal religion; found a narrow-minded ceremonial, and originated a spiritual principle; I can do nothing but reply, that every one of those statements is groundless and contrary to fact[s]." "'Tis quite incredible," he adds in another passage, "that Jesus ever taught His disciples the religious nullity of Levitical ordinances, the equality of Gentiles with Jews before God[t]." But mark, I pray you, on how slight a basis these vehement and sweeping assertions rest. "What His disciples never understood Him to teach," it is argued, "He certainly did not teach effectively[u]." But the objector overlooks what surely he would be one of the last to deny, that the greatest truths can only be imparted gradually; that the earliest stage in the acceptance of them is often, if not always, unconscious; that the highest teaching is not that which communicates certain formulæ, but that which deposits in the mind a seed hereafter to bear fruit a hundredfold; not that which loads the memory, but that which quickens the apprehension; not that which imparts the thing to be learnt, but that which imparts the power of learning. True, the disciples did not understand their Master's meaning at the time. How should they? If when He told them of earthly things, of the common duties of daily life, of forgiving one another, and so forth, they were dull of hearing, how could they fathom His thoughts when He spoke of a divine love, wide as

[s] F. W. Newman, *Against Hero-making in Religion*, p. 23.
[t] Ibid., p. 11.   [u] Ibid., p. 23.

the canopy of heaven, embracing all races and lands without distinction? Yet even they, these same disciples, so slow of understanding, had learnt the meaning of His words, when immediately after His departure from them they admitted a Roman centurion into their communion. When Christ Jesus cancelled the prescriptive and exclusive claim of Abraham's seed to be the children of God, He virtually abolished the exclusiveness of privilege everywhere. When He announced, "I, if I be lifted up, will draw all men to Me[x]," and when He commanded His bereaved and bewildered followers to "go and teach all nations[y]," He established "a brotherhood of man and an equality of races[z]" which neither the barbaric turbulence of feudal ages, nor the more subtle disintegration of modern luxury, can ever nullify. The very gradualness of the change that came over the world is the most wonderful thing about it. Not by convulsive tremblings of the earth, as when the rocks of Horeb in the thick darkness were rent by the clang of the trumpet, but by the almost imperceptible subsidence, age after age, of the barriers of caste and faction, at the still small voice of Evangelic morality, will the prophetic word sometime be accomplished: "Every valley shall be exalted, and every mountain shall be brought low[a]," and "all nations of the earth shall be blessed in Him[b]," who came, and lived, and died, and rose again, and lives for ever for all.

[x] St. John xii. 32.   [y] St. Matt. xxviii. 19.   [z] F. W. Newman, *v. supra.*   [a] St. Luke iii. 5.   [b] Gen. xxiii. 18.

LECTURE VII.
Alleged Defects of Christian Morality.

ST. MATTHEW xi. 19.

"*Wisdom is justified of her children.*"

I HAVE reserved for separate consideration some special objections to Christian morality, which might naturally have attached themselves to one or other of the previous Lectures, because they require more attention than could be given in passing.

Such, for instance, is the objection, with which we are familiar, that Christianity, after more than fifteen centuries of ascendancy in Europe, still permits war, that self-inflicted scourge of our race, to disgrace our civilization and our religion; nay, that the carnage is multiplied tenfold. What shall we say in reply?

The latter part of the objection is not to the point. If, as time goes on, the ingenuity of science can invent instruments of slaughter more and more destructive, if the ponderous artillery and keen-sighted rifle of our day deal death farther and wider than the mediæval cross-bow or the sharpened flint of a yet ruder age, this is simply an affair of mechanics, of progress in material science. Nay, some will say that these increased facilities of killing make war less frequent, and that in proportion as the havoc and misery which it causes are seen and felt on a larger scale, nations are less likely to have recourse to it.

But this is not the real question at issue, as regards Christianity. For, as we can scarcely be reminded too often, in attempting a moral comparison between one age or one country and another, size, bulk, extent are not everything. The real horrors of war may be felt as much in the skirmishings of a savage tribe as in the colossal campaigns of a Napoleon. It is not the number of lives which they cost, but the temper in which they are conducted, that marks the difference between one war and another in morality. Now it cannot be denied that from being the normal state of nations, hostile because neighbouring, war, under the influence of Christianity, is becoming a last resource after other ways of settling a dispute have failed. The moral sense of Christendom, though at times corrupted by the sophistries of ambition, or intimidated by huge battalions, still, as a rule, pronounces unequivocally against the aggressor. Whatever may be urged, and with reason, against war in general, or more particularly against the "perpetual menace" of standing armies, war must remain to the end of time a necessity, so long as human nature, even with religion to elevate and purify it, remains what it is. In fact, the soldier holds among nations something like the office of the policeman among individuals; and the utmost that the most sanguine may dare to hope is, that the appeal to arms may become less and less frequent of occurrence, and that public opinion may side more and more strongly with those who fight on the defensive. That much has been done already no impartial student of history will deny, if he compares Europe as it was in the fifth century with what it is in our time, who have just seen what might have been an internecine struggle bloodlessly terminated by arbitration. We have seen, too, how the horrors of war, even of war on a Titanic scale, may be alleviated by a growing respect for the lives and property of non-combatants, and by the devoted labours of Christian men and women, ready to relieve the sufferings on either side.

We must throw ourselves back in thought from our own more peaceful life to the day when the vast amphitheatres of the capital of the civilized world were thronged with spectators, not a few of them ladies of rank and culture, to see hired swordmen butcher one another in cold blood; or to the older time, when human sacrifices reeked on the altar [a]. True — this "sense" "of the sanctity of human life [b]" did not arrive at maturity all at once. The world was not to be roused from its trance to a new consciousness rudely and suddenly, but by a gentle hand. By slow degrees the warring states of Europe were welded into the confederacy which we call Christendom, and war came to be considered not so much a trial of brute force as a kind of ordeal, an appeal to the God of Right; and its ferocity was tempered by the interchange of knightly courtesies. In the

[a] Euripides, *Hecub.*, 40, 41.
[b] Lecky, *History of European Morals*, ii. 19.

far West, at the preaching of Christian missionaries, women were freed for ever from the revolting obligation of military service, with its stain of blood[c]; and if Christianity could not persuade the warlike spirit of the Franks to "beat their swords into ploughshares, and their spears into pruning-hooks," it persuaded them to keep, as it were, a periodical Sabbath from their feuds, a peace, or, at least, a truce of God[d]. The leaven has done, is doing, its work. It has leavened, is leavening, the world.

So, again, as regards slavery: Christianity is reproached that it did not abolish and efface slavery summarily. Indeed, it is strange, at the first glance, to read of a public slave-mart in Rome so late as the sixth century of our era, and of ecclesiastics quietly standing by, apparently without a word of protest against the traffic in flesh and blood. But, it must be repeated, the aim, the purport of the Gospel was not to revolutionise society, was not to effect a forcible revulsion in human nature, but to train and discipline it, as only it can be trained and disciplined, gradually, or rather to help it to train and discipline itself. If Christianity had attempted at one blow to liberate the myriads of slaves within the Roman Empire, this would have been to proclaim a servile war, a sanguinary uprising against order and property. And the attempt must have failed, because premature, because the world was not ready for it. But the humanising influence of Christianity was at

[c] By the Lex Adamnani.
[d] In the early part of the eleventh century.

work continually to alleviate the evil[e], and to prepare the way for its extinction. In the principles which it enunciated so unfalteringly, Christianity was applying a solvent to the manacles of the slave, so that, in the ripeness of time, they should fall from his wrists at the voice of a Clarkson or a Wilberforce. Even from the very first Christianity welcomed the slave to her arms, and told him of an emancipation commencing on earth, but to be consummated in heaven. Once admitted to the Christian Covenant, the slave became the freedman of Christ, and "a citizen of no mean city," a citizen of the city of God. As an adopted son of God, he could henceforth claim not equality merely, but brotherhood, with the greatest earthly potentates. For in Christ is "neither bond nor free[f]."

To say, "there is no protest" in the Gospel of Christ "against slavery[g]," is to shut one's eyes to its constant assertion of the perfect equality in God's sight of all races and conditions of men, of the inherent, the indefeasible rights and responsibilities of each person separately[h].

Yes! some will reply, Christianity does recognise, and even exaggerate, what is due to each person singly and solely, but it fails to recognise what is due from each to the community of which he is

[e] Before the introduction of Christianity, even the Saxons, with their strong domestic instincts, sold their own flesh and blood.—Cf. Montalembert, *Monks of the West*, iii. 327.

[f] Gal. iii. 28.

[g] F. W. Newman, *On the Defective Morality of the New Testament*, p. 20.   [h] See Note D.

a member; an obligation, the greatness of which is instinctively attested when we speak of the individual as belonging to the community, not of the community as belonging to him. "In Pagan Ethics," it is justly remarked, this duty of the citizen to the State had even a "disproportionate" value attached to it, so as to "infringe on the just liberty of the individual." "In purely Christian Ethics," the writer adds, less justly, "it is scarcely noticed or acknowledged[i]." And yet the very context of these words suggests, in part at least, their refutation; for almost in the same sentence Christianity is accused of unduly magnifying the duty of obedience, of setting up "a standard of ethics, in which the only worth professedly recognised is obedience[j]." But obedience, the habit, that is, of deference to law or authority, of postponing private predilections, private convictions, private advantage to the public good, is an important element in the patriotism which makes a nation march as one man, and which sacrifices, if it must be, the dearest interests of self to the welfare of the community. But let us look closer. What is patriotism? whence its origin? what the fundamental principle which it rests upon? Patriotism is the development of the love of home, even as the State is the development of the family. And the home, the family, depends, not for its stability only but for its existence, on that reverence for the sanctity of marriage which is allowed on all sides, in praise or in blame, to be an essential attribute of

[i] J. S. Mill, *On Liberty*, p. 29.   [j] Ibid.

Christianity[k]. Take away this, annul the strictness, the permanency of the marriage-bond, the mutual fidelity of man and wife, and, as the family loses its cohesion, so, more slowly indeed but not less surely, the state is broken up, falls to pieces, crumbles away into nothing; and mankind relapses, from the ennobling organizations of the city and of the nation, into the chaos of savagery, into the promiscuous herding together of beasts. Have we not ourselves witnessed very lately the frantic efforts of an anti-social cosmopolitanism to sweep away the partitions which Christianity has sanctioned between nation and nation, and between home and home?

The objection takes a wider range. "The ideal of Christian morality" is represented as "negative and passive," its virtue as "innocence rather than nobleness; abstinence from evil rather than the energetic pursuit of good[l]." Can these words, indeed, be written of the morality of the Gospel? Is not the writer thinking of that older, narrower code, which Christ came to expand and to vivify, when he gravely tells us "'Thou shalt not' predominates over 'Thou shalt;'" thinking of some fanatical perversion of Christianity by a Manes, a Calvin, or an Antony of the desert, when he describes the Christian type of character as a "low and abject type of character, which submits to what it deems the Divine Will, but cannot rise to the conception of the Divine Goodness[m]." Take the Sermon on the Mount and

---

[k] See Lecture III., pp. 43—45.   [l] J. S. Mill, *On Liberty*, p. 28.   [m] Ibid., p. 30.

the other discourses of our Lord. The burden of them is this, that men are to rise above the slavish timidity which shrinks from doing good in its dread of doing evil to a spirit of beneficence, wide as earth and high as heaven. Take the parables of our Lord. Few, very few, but embody, in one shape or another, this truth, that he who folds his hands and stands aloof from the great conflict of good and evil, is a recreant to his Lord. Take the foreshadowings of future judgment. The verdict of acquittal or of condemnation turns on this, "What hast thou done with thy time, thy talents, thy opportunities? What noble, unselfish purpose hast thou turned them to[n]?" And the crown of victory is not for him who declines temptation, but who overcomes it[o]. Take the life and death of Him who is to us Example as well as Teacher, Example as well as Mediator. The keynote of His Life, of His Ministry, of His Passion, in His own words is this: "I have a work to do, and how am I straitened, till it be accomplished[p];" "I must be about My Father's business[q];" "I must undo the works of Satan[r];" "I must do the works of Him that sent Me;" "the night cometh, when no man can work[s];" "I am come to send fire on the earth; and what will I, if it be already kindled[t]." The charge of inertness or passivity is certainly a strange one to bring against Christianity.

It is admitted that "the sayings of Christ are irre-

[n] e.g. St. Matt. xxv. 40. [o] Rev. iii. 21; St. James i. 12.
[p] St. Luke xii. 50. [q] Ibid. ii. 49. [r] e.g. Ibid. xiii. 16.
[s] St. John ix. 4; cf. Ibid. vii. 7, xvii. 4. [t] St. Luke xii. 49.

concilable with nothing which a comprehensive morality requires;" and that "everything excellent in ethics may be brought within them ᵘ." And yet it is objected that they "contain only part of the truth, and omit many essential elements of the highest morality ˣ." It has been the object of these Lectures to shew, that no "essential element of morality" is omitted in Christianity, but that all "the essential elements of the highest morality" are found there in a fulness and with a harmony which are absolutely unique. At the same time it has been admitted, or rather it has been urged very earnestly, that these "elements of morality" are to be looked for in the Gospel of Christ in an "elemental" form. To say that "the Gospel of Christ is not a complete morality," and that "it is corrective of a pre-existent morality ʸ," is in effect a repetition of our Lord's own words, "I am not come to destroy, but to fulfil ᶻ." To say that Christian morality "must be eked out from the Old Testament," that "it is incomplete without secular standards," and that "St. Paul ekes it out from the Greeks and Romans ᵃ," is no disparagement, but in strict accordance with our Lord's retrospective allusions to the law of Moses ᵇ, and to St. Paul's appeal to nature ᶜ and conscience ᵈ, as a proof that the Father of all never left Himself without a witness ᵉ. To say that the morality of the

ᵘ J. S. Mill, *On Liberty*, p. 29.   ˣ Ibid.   ʸ Ibid., p. 28.
ᶻ St. Matt. v. 17.   ᵃ J. S. Mill, *On Liberty*, p. 28.   ᵇ St. Luke xvi. 16.   ᶜ e.g. Acts xiv. 15.   ᵈ e.g. Ibid. xvii. 28.   ᵉ Ibid. xiv. 17.

Gospel is couched in "terms most general," and that Christian morality, as we have it, is "not the work of Christ or of His Apostles[f]," but the growth of centuries, is in other words to admit, as we contend, that the principles of the Gospel are contained in the Gospel implicitly rather than explicitly; that they are not fossilised petrifactions, but living, fructifying principles; that they are so framed in order to elicit and stimulate in the heart a living, fructifying principle of action; and that by their very nature, by this their capacity of testing what is genuine in man and what is false, they are themselves capable of perversion[g].

One more objection, — and yet it scarcely needs an answer, especially here in a Christian University, which has been a centre of light to Europe in the twilight of an imperfect civilization, and which claims, by its very title, to encourage and direct the pursuit of knowledge of every sort and kind. Christianity is accused of being hostile or indifferent to knowledge. Because in Christian education the first and foremost thing is godliness,—and I need not stop to remind you that godliness, as the word reminds us, is the development in man of a likeness to the wisdom and majesty which are the attributes of God;—therefore, yet most illogically, it is argued, "Christian education is *only* in the nurture and admonition of the Lord[h]." Because St. Paul exalts charity, that is, self-sacrificing

---

[f] J. S. Mill, *On Liberty*, p. 28.   [g] See Note E.

[h] F. W. Newman, *On the Defective Morality of the New Testament*, p. 32.

love, above a mere intellectual proficiency, therefore we are told, "Knowledge is only sarcastically glanced at in the New Testament[i]." And though this greatest of Christian teachers, while exhorting his converts to be "children" in guilelessness, adds in his very next words, "in understanding be ye men[k];" though he charges them to be earnest and diligent in the pursuit "of whatsoever things are lovely, and of good report[l];" though he insists that "every good gift," every capacity, faculty, accomplishment of man's being, is "from above, from the Father of lights[m]," nor scruples to make his appeal freely to the secular literature of the Gentile world; though, to pass from the disciple to the Master, our Lord Himself has taught us, by parable and by precept[n], that we are all responsible for the improvement and use of every talent entrusted to our keeping; yet, in the face of all this, the sceptic writes, "That knowledge deserves to be studied for its own sake, that the desire of knowledge is a virtue, no hint is given in Scripture[o]." Yet more: "If the New Testament," he adds, "is not hostile to this faculty," (he is speaking of the sense of beauty,) "its silence is a grave defect." Does an accusation like this need a reply? To take at hazard one instance out of many. Can we forget whose Voice has bidden the children of men, troubled and disquieted in vain with sordid

---

[i] F. W. Newman, *On the Defective Morality of the New Testament*, p. 29.   [k] 1 Cor. xiv. 20.   [l] Phil. iv. 8.   [m] St. James i. 17.   [n] e.g. In the parable of the Slothful Servant.   [o] F. W. Newman, *On the Defective Morality of the New Testament*, p. 29.

H

cares, to turn their weary eyes to the flowers which fringe their path, to " consider the lilies of the field, how they grow [p]," and to rejoice in the beauty of the universe, even in its minutest features. Even were it true, this alleged silence of the New Testament on the sense of beauty, the arts which Christianity has fostered would speak to confute the cavil. The glowing canvasses of Italy or of Spain, the stately towers and spires of northern minsters, the thrilling harmonies of Handel or of Bach,—these are our answer to the objector who accuses our faith of discouraging art, or of deadening the sense of beauty.

[p] St. Matt. vi. 28.

LECTURE VIII.
Summary and Conclusion.

ST. MATTHEW xxvii. 54.

" Truly this was the Son of God."

IT has been the endeavour of these Lectures to set before you some of those characteristics of Christian Morality which mark it off from other systems, as purer and loftier than they. How imperfectly the design which I proposed to myself has been accomplished, I am well aware. But I am not without hope that others, more competent than I, may be induced to prosecute the line of thought here suggested, and to elaborate what is but a sketch into the fulness and exactness of a finished picture. For in the moral characteristics of Christianity we have a foundation for our faith, deep as the innermost conscience of man, and wide as the earth's circumference [a].

Let me ask you to retrace very cursorily the steps of our argument.

First, something was said with a view to assuring ourselves that there is really any such thing as an acknowledged standard of right and wrong, speaking morally. For even this may not pass unchallenged; not a few, like Pilate, asking sadly or scoffingly,

[a] See Note F.

"What is truth?" Next, an attempt was made to shew, mainly on psychological grounds, that the vital principle of moral excellence in its every phase is unselfish love, the principle of vice, selfishness.

So far our enquiry was preliminary. The next stage in it was to test the moral teaching of the Gospel by this rule, classifying our desires, as they find their gratification in the pleasures of sense, in the exercise of power over others, or in the pure consciousness of superiority. Lastly, I called your attention to the breadth and elasticity of the evangelic morality, and essayed to reply to some noteworthy objections to it, as defective and faulty. I think I am not overstating the case in favour of Christianity, nor doing injustice to other types of moral excellence, if I say, that we find a purity, a tenderness, an integrity in Christian morals, in one word, an unselfishness, which we seek in vain elsewhere.

Are we to stop here? If, indeed, we are persuaded that Christ Jesus inculcated a holier rule of conduct than any other teacher, while by His life and death He gave to the world an example of entire self-sacrifice such as it has never seen before or since, can we stop short of the irresistible conclusion, that the Teacher and the Teaching are divine? Can we refrain from exclaiming with the eyewitness of His sufferings on the Cross, "Truly this was the Son of God?" In these sublime precepts, in this reproachless life of untiring beneficence, in this unfaltering self-devotion from the cradle at Bethlehem to the Cross on Calvary, have we not found what the sceptic defies us to find—I borrow his words—" One who dwarfs all others before and after Him, one to whose high sympathy sages and prophets must bow[a]," One—will you not add with me?—who wins our love, as the Son of Man, who claims our adoration, as the Son of God most high?

Let it be remembered, that the moral teaching of Christianity and the great fundamental doctrines of the Christian faith, are very closely linked together. For reasons given in an earlier Lecture, to avoid complicating our enquiry, or seeming to anticipate our conclusion, I have purposely refrained from mixing theology with morality. And yet I have felt all along, as doubtless you have felt with me, and I have not hesitated to give expression to the feeling, that whatever there is of best and noblest in the morality of the Gospel, flows as of necessity from the great facts of theology which the Gospel reveals. Love or unselfishness, it matters not which name we choose, is, if we have reasoned rightly, that which sums up in itself the characteristics of Christian practice. And what else than love is the substance and the purport of a Creed, which tells us of a Father of all, who "spared not His Only Son for men[b];" of a Saviour, who left heaven to save the helpless; of a Holy Spirit, ever aiding the vacillating wills of men to reject the evil and to choose the good? Why there should be evil in the universe, why man, above other creatures, should be invested with this

[a] F. W. Newman, *Against Hero-making in Religion*, p. 8.
[b] Rom. viii. 32.

awful prerogative of being free to choose good or evil, life or death, is not our question. The existence of evil is a fact, which must be accepted as a starting-point in all our surmisings. But so much as this at least must be allowed. Granted, that evil is, and must be by the conditions of our nature, no system of philosophy or of theology throws so strong a light on the disciplinary character of evil, or supplies to men so strong a motive for overcoming it, as the Creed of Christendom in its purest, simplest form.

In our attempt to form a just estimate of Christian morality, reference has been made to results; for, if discriminated fairly, its results tell strongly for or against a creed. But, after all, "it is a shallow philosophy"—I borrow, again, the words of an opponent of Christianity—"to measure a hero not by what he is, but by what he has done[c]." It is well said. For the hindrances in the way of those who desire to do good service to the Truth are great and manifold. If the amount of good done by Christianity in the world seems far less than was to be expected, I pray you to listen to the words, as wise as they are eloquent, which we owe to the pen of one whom this University numbers with pride among her sons, words written of the apparently very partial success which attended the labours of an eminent Church reformer in the eleventh century, but which are true also of the apparently inadequate success of Christianity in its attempt to regenerate the world: "What are all reforms, restorations, victories of

[c] F. W. Newman, *Against Hero-making in Religion*, p. 7.

truth, but protests of a minority; efforts, clogged and incomplete, of the good and brave; just enough in their own day to stop instant ruin, the appointed means to save what is to be saved, but in themselves failures. Good men work and suffer, and bad men enjoy their labours and spoil them; a step is made in advance —evil rolled back and kept in check for a time, only to return perhaps the stronger. But thus, and thus only, is truth passed on, and the world preserved from utter corruption[d]." Why this should be, why decay and corruption should thus impress their seal, as on all forms of outward beauty, so on all that is fairest and noblest morally,—why, with efforts so strenuous, so unremitting in every age on the part of the brave and true to force back the tide of evil, its crested waves seem ever and anon as though they would submerge the earth,—this we ask in vain. But let me ask of you two questions, which are not beyond our scope to answer,—What other force is there in the world which makes even an attempt to contend with evil, moral and physical, as Christianity does? And what would our life, our collective life, the life of each one singly, be, if the light of love which the Gospel sheds upon it were, indeed, quenched and gone, if the Sun of Righteousness were blotted out of our firmament, if the salt of Christian holiness were, indeed, to lose its savour?

There are some, not a few, especially among the educated and the intellectual, who put questions like

[d] R. W. Church, *St. Anselm*, p. 294.

these aside, as if no answer need be given one way or the other. When Agrippa was told of "one Jesus, which was dead, whom Paul affirmed to be alive," his reply was this, "I would hear the man myself[e]." He would not prejudge a question so startling and so momentous, without at any rate hearing what Paul had to say about it. But now, when we are told that He who died on Calvary is "risen indeed[f]," and "lives for evermore[g]," and "holds the keys of hell and death[h]," and is "mighty to save[i]," not a few turn away with an indifference which cares neither to affirm nor to deny, as if the convictions, which changed the whole life-course of a man like Saul of Tarsus, were not worth a moment's consideration. We, in our day, seem so far removed from the events of the Gospel history: the Voice of which those who heard it said, "He speaks as never man spake[j]," reaches our ears faintly and from far away, through the intervening centuries; it is well-nigh lost amid the angry recriminations of our controversies. Like the Israelites waiting for the return of their leader from the summit of Sinai, men are tempted to say in their hearts, "We wot not what is become of Him[k]" who promised to return so speedily. Men ask, longingly or in scorn, "Why tarry the wheels of His chariot?" why sleeps that trumpet of the Archangel which is to wake the dead to meet the Advent of their Lord? Nay, Christians, let us look back through the mist of years, and see in thought the gracious form of the

[e] Acts xxv. 22. [f] St. Luke xxiv. 24. [g] Rev. i. 18.
[h] Ibid. [i] Isa. lxiii. 1. [j] St. John vii. 46. [k] Acts vii. 40.

Son of Man, as He "went about doing good[1]." Let us listen eagerly, amid the harsher sounds of earth, for the Voice which says, "Come unto Me, all ye that labour and are heavy laden, and I will give you rest[m]." Let us believe Him, as He invites us to do, "for His works' sake[n]." If we believe that Jesus taught, lived, died, as the Gospels pourtray Him teaching, living, dying, then to believe that He worked miracles, rose from the grave, went up into heaven, follows as of course. "O! Arm of the Lord, art thou not it that hath cut Rahab, and wounded the dragon? Art thou not it, which hath dried the sea, the waters of the great deep; that hath made the depths of the sea a way for the redeemed to pass over[o]?" O! Arm of Christ our Lord, art Thou not it, which overcame Sin and Death on the Cross, which made a way for His redeemed to pass through the waters of death safely?

To wait, in suspense, in uncertainty, is in one sense the attitude of a believer in Christ Jesus. For we "know not the day, nor the hour of His coming;" and till He comes, our clearest vision only sees "through a glass darkly," our largest knowledge only "knows in part[p]." If faith were certainty, it would cease to be a probation. If it could be demonstrated to the intellect, it would cease to appeal, as it does, to our appreciation of right and wrong morally; would cease to be a criterion, whether we love self best, or something worthier. In this sense

---

[1] Acts x. 38.   [m] St. Matt. xi. 28.   [n] St. John xiv. 11.
[o] Isa. li. 9.   [p] 1 Cor. xiii. 13.

a Christian waits, with a lifelong waiting, for the solution of the insoluble, for the attainment of what is here beyond attainment; waits, well content to leave many a question unanswered in this life, that he would fain have answered, if it were possible. In this sense, to "wait" is the Christian's watchword amid his perplexities.

But in another sense, to wait, undecided and inert, to sit on the bank, counting the ripples of Time's stream as it glides past, while we ought to be borne onward on its waters to fresh hopes and fresh exertions, to stand "idle in the market-place" while the others are "bearing the heat and burden of the day" is folly and ingratitude. It is folly, if, while in other matters we are daily, hourly acting on what is mere probability[q], we turn away from the Christ till we can have proof positive that He is what He claims to be. It is ingratitude of the basest, if the trouble and the responsibility of enquiry deter us from facing the question,—Is it or is it not the truth, that this All-holy Being lived and died for me? O! you who have yet your lives before you, whose future has as yet no wasted past to sigh for, believe me, to put off the earnest consideration of these things, is not only to let slip time which can never be recalled, it is to weave round yourselves a tangled mesh of habit which will take years to unravel; it is to sully the crystal of your souls with a stain, which some day you shall be fain to wash away, if it may be, with tears. "How long halt ye between two opinions?"

[q] Cf. Bishop Butler's Analogy.

If Christ be God, then follow Him. If the blind forces of a material mechanism be God,——but I will not finish the sentence. "Blessed is he that waiteth [r]," so the exiled seer comforted his soul in the dark days of the captivity,—"Blessed is he that waiteth," not holding back his hand from the work that cries out to be done,—the work to which our Lord leads us on,—the work of undoing, day by day, the works of darkness—till every subtle question that can be devised has been laid to rest; but working on, in faith, in patience—even with but a scanty light on his endeavours. Blessed they, who shall be able to say at last, "This is our God, we have waited for Him, and He will save us [s];" for, while we saw Him not, "His statutes have been our song in the house of our pilgrimage [t]."

[r] Dan. xii. 12.   [s] Isa. xxv. 9.   [t] Ps. cxix. 54.

APPENDIX.

NOTE A.

See Lecture I., p. 12.

It seems difficult, even for those most conversant with the Talmud, to pronounce positively, how far its loftiest flights of morality are really independent of Christianity. "We do not believe," says a recent learned writer on the Talmud, "that we have it" (the Mishna) "in its original shape."—*Quarterly Review*, ccxlvi. p. 442. "They" (the MSS.) "are only fragmentary for the most part," p. 421.

"The Canonical books" (of Buddhism) belong "to a much later period" (than 550 B.C.)—M. Müller, *Buddhism*, p. 4.

How far the philosophy of Imperial Rome was affected by the new religion emanating from Judæa, and making its converts in the first century there, as elsewhere, is discussed by Mr. Lecky in his interesting *History of European Morals* (i. 361, 2). "The greatest moralists of the Roman Empire never mentioned Christianity, or mentioned it with contempt; they habitually disregarded the many religions that had arisen among the ignorant; and we have no direct evidence of the slightest value of their having come into contact with, or favoured the Christians." Still, even granting this, it does not follow that the leavening influence of Christianity was not silently at work in the schools of philosophy as in the court of the Cæsars, (cf. Philippians iv. 22.) Mr. G. Long (*M. Aurelius Antoninus*, p. 22) thinks that "the Emperor knew nothing of Christianity." On the other hand, see *Il Christianesimo nascente* (by Il Conte Tullio Dandolo); Champagny, *Les Antonins;* Tillemont, *Histoire des Empereurs* (tom. ii.) and *Mémoires* (tom. ii. art. ii.); Allies, *The Formation of Christendom;* Fleury, *Les*

Mœurs des Chrétiens; Mamachi, *Costumi dei primitivi Christiani;* Döllinger, *Introduction to History of Christianity;* Turretin, *Traité de la Verité de la Religion Chrétienne;* and the *Bibliothèque Sacrée,* by the Dominicans, Richard and Geraud (s. v. Religion). For these references, I am indebted to the learned Rev. J. Skinner, M.A., Vicar of Newland.

NOTE B.

See Lecture II., p. 22.

MORAL AVERAGES.

It is sometimes argued that the existence of Free-will in man is inconsistent with statistical results, which, it is said, shew, or tend to shew, that his actions may be reduced to fixed or slightly-varying averages, and are therefore, it is argued, governed, like other natural phenomena, by fixed, invariable, inevitable laws.

Assuming, for the moment, that the uniformity of such averages is truly stated, it may be answered,—

(1.) So far as they relate to acts which result from the physical condition of man, they prove nothing as to the freedom of the Will. Even as regards moral action, so far as other than moral causes intervene, these may disturb the result, and the apparent constancy of the average may only shew that the Will has to work with implements and under conditions which limit its freedom, and give a fixity to its operations which does not belong to the Will itself.

(2.) Free-agency is not the same thing as mere lawless caprice of Will[a]. Independently of circumstances which rouse the moral sense into action, either in the individual or in masses of people, a sudden change for better or worse is not to be expected. It is enough for the advocate of free-agency if such a change follows the infusion into society of fresh moral elements, such, for instance, as a Christian believes to have been revealed in the Person and teaching of Christ.

[a] Religion and Science alike recognise Law in Nature; the Law, to many minds, implying a Lawgiver.

But it may be questioned whether any such fixed average of moral action can be shewn to exist as is required to support even a probable argument against the freedom of the Will.

To take for illustration a single class of crimes committed in this country, it appears from the last published Judicial Statistics [b] of England and Wales that the total number of murders reported by the police in the year 1870-1 was 130 as against 101 in 1869-70; or, allowing for the increase of population, 1 in 174,647 for the year 1870-1, against 1 in 218,714 for the year 1869-70; 1 in 144,831 for the year 1868-9; 1 in 167,824 for 1867-8; and 1 in 158,737 for 1866-7; numbers which are only slightly altered, not reduced to any regular average, by including the attempts to murder also. Thus in 1870-1 the attempts to murder were 51, as against 52 in 1869-70, the proportion of such offences to the population being—

For the year 1870-1, 1 to 445,178.
,,   1869-70, 1 to 424,810.
,,   1868-9, 1 to 358,515.
,,   1867-8, 1 to 354,907.
,,   1866-7, 1 to 476,211.

So, again, the total number of persons summarily proceeded against for drunkenness, or as being drunk or disorderly, for each year from 1866-7 to 1870-1 is returned as follows [c]:—

1870-1.	1869-70.	1868-9.	1867-8.	1866-7.
142,343	131,870	122,310.	111,465.	100,357.

Once more, it has been stated [d] that the number of sentences of penal servitude, which in the year 1830 had been

---

[b] Judicial Statistics, 1871, England and Wales, Part I., p. xiv.

[c] Ibid., p. xviii. These figures I owe to my brother, John George Smith, M.A., Barrister-at-Law.

[d] By the Home Secretary, Mr. Bruce, in moving the Second Reading of the Prevention of Crime Bill, Feb., 1873, as reported in the *Times*, Feb. 21.

upwards of 4,100, fell, in 1869, to 2,006; in 1870, to 1,788; in 1871, to 1,628; and in 1872, to 1,494, shewing in the last four years, with an increasing population, a reduction of 25 per cent.

These numbers may, of course, have been largely affected by legislation, police administration, and innumerable other causes; but it should be remembered that legislative Acts are in great measure an embodiment of the moral feeling of the community. At any rate, the wide variation in the number of crimes committed from year to year tends to shew that no such regularity of average has been established as will avail for logical proof.

Moreover, if we take a wider view over a longer course of time, is it not an acknowledged fact, that the moral characteristics of the same nation have varied; that one kind of vice prevails in one age, another in another; that the moral habits of a community are inextricably interwoven with social customs and positive laws, which again are the combined product of moral and material causes; that the very frequency and excess of a particular crime or vice in one age may lead to its mitigation or repression by the force of public opinion, acting through positive law or social custom, in another?

Also, the moral state of a community is dependent, more or less directly, upon material conditions, such as war and peace, plentiful or deficient harvests, prosperity or depression of trade, &c.

All this, of course, is not any proof that the Will is free, but it seems to be destructive of the argument against its freedom derived from the supposed constancy of averages.

But perhaps it may be said, abandoning the argument from the constancy or regularity of averages, that the fact that moral acts and habits *are* dependent upon these various influences, social, legislative, and material, is the very proof required that they are no more the result of free agency than any other facts of human nature; and that, although by a sort of transmutation of moral forces (like that resulting from the "correlation" of physical forces in natural science) morality assumes different phases in different periods, one kind of vice or habit passing into another, and so on, there exists from first to last a constant, invariable quantity, or force, of so-called moral evil, which the so-called Will is powerless to destroy or eliminate.

But it seems enough to answer, that this is a theory too vague and impalpable to admit of any scientific test; although on a general view, e.g. of the state of Europe before and after the diffusion of Christianity, the moral difference may to an unbiassed mind be amply apparent.

In fact, it would seem to be a hopeless attempt to prove or disprove the freedom of the Will, by registering the outward acts of men taken in the mass. Is it not the more scientific course to study the operations of the Will, not where they are complicated a thousand-fold with motives and causes which affect its action, and yet cannot by any analysis be eliminated, but rather, after the old ethical method, where it may be examined in its simplest and purest form, in the inward workings of the consciousness of each man, and in the outward experiences of individualistic action? For such purposes there is little likelihood that the old science of Ethics will ever be superseded by Sociology.

NOTE C.

See Lecture VI., p. 78.

Self-murder has been dignified with the euphemistic title of Euthanasia. The question of it being right or wrong, speaking generally and without reference to particular instances, turns on the same hinge as the whole argument of these Lectures. Is a man's life his own property, or is it a trust in his keeping for his God and his fellows? In the one case, he can fairly ask, "May I not do what I will with mine own?" In the other case, the responsibility of abruptly terminating it by his own act can only, if ever, be justified by very extreme circumstances.

NOTE D.

See Lecture VII., p. 91.

"Of no idea is it so generally known that it is indefinite, ambiguous, liable to the greatest misconstructions, and, in reality, consequently subjected to them, than of the idea of free-will, and none is in current use, with so little intelligence. But, as we may express ourselves, the *free* spirit being the *actual existent* spirit, or the spirit that actually prevails in human affairs being the spirit of free-will, misconstructions in regard to it are of the most enormous consequence. For when persons and peoples are once for all possessed by the abstract notion of freedom as such, freedom on its own account, no other has such irresistible power, and just because it is the very inmost being of spirit, its very actuality and self. Entire quarters of the globe, Africa, and the East, have never had, and have not yet this idea. The Greeks and Romans, Plato and Aristotle and the Stoics, had it not. On the contrary, they conceived only that a man by his birth (as Athenian or Spartan citizen, &c.), or by strength of character, by education, by philosophy (the wise man is free even when a slave or in chains), only so did they conceive a man to be free. This idea came into the world through Christianity, in which it is that the individual, *as such*, has an *infinite* worth, as being aim and object of the love of God, and destined, consequently, to have his absolute relation to God as spirit, to have this spirit dwelling in him. Christianity it was, namely, that revealed man in *himself* to be destined to supreme freedom. . . . . This idea, then, is the very actuality of man, and not that he *has* it, but that he *is* it.

"Christianity has made it the very actuality of its adherents,—the very actuality of its adherents,—not to be a slave, for example. If reduced to slavery, if the control over their property is to depend on caprice, and not on laws and courts of justice, then they find the very substance of their being violated. This volition of freedom is no longer an impulse, an instinct that demands its gratification; it is now a *character*,—a spiritual consciousness that is above impulse, that is above instinct. But this freedom, this free-will, and free-agency, that possesses such implement, such filling, such aims and ends, cannot remain as notion only, as mere principle of the mind or the heart. It must unclose itself into objectivity—into an organic actuality, legal, moral, political, and religious."—Hegel, *Philosophie des Geistes*, p. 374; quoted by J. H. Stirling, *Lectures on the Philosophy of Law*, pp. 27, 28.

NOTE E.

See Lecture VII., p. 96.

"To what an extent doctrines intrinsically fitted to make the deepest impression upon the mind may remain in it as dead beliefs, without being ever realized in the imagination, the feelings, or the understanding, is exemplified by the manner in which the majority of believers hold the doctrines of Christianity. By Christianity I here mean what is accounted such by all churches and sects,—the maxims and precepts contained in the New Testament. These are considered sacred, and accepted as laws, by all professing Christians. Yet it is scarcely too much to say that not one Christian in a thousand guides or tests his individual conduct by reference to those laws. The standard, to which he does refer it, is the custom of his nation, his class, or his religious profession. He has thus, on the one hand, a collection of ethical maxims, which he believes to have been vouchsafed to him by infallible wisdom as rules for his government; and on the other, a set of every-day judgments and practices, which go a certain length with some of those maxims, not so great a length with others, stand in direct opposition to some, and are, on the whole, a compromise between the Christian creed and the interests and suggestions of worldly life. To the first of these standards he gives his homage; to the other his real allegiance. All Christians believe that the blessed are the poor and humble, and those who are ill-used by the world; that it is easier for a camel to pass through the eye of a needle than for a rich man to enter the kingdom of heaven; that they should judge not, lest they be judged; that they should swear not at all; that they should love their neighbour as themselves; that if one take their cloak, they should give him their coat also; that they should take no thought for the morrow; that if they would be perfect, they should sell all that they have and give it to the poor. They are not insincere when they say that they believe these things; they do believe them, as people believe what they have always heard lauded and never discussed. But in the sense of that living belief which regulates conduct, they believe these doctrines just up to the point to which it is usual to act upon them. The doctrines in their integrity are serviceable to pelt adversaries with; and it is understood that they are to be put forward (when possible) as the reasons for whatever people do that they think laudable. But any one who reminded them that the maxims require an infinity of things which they never even think of doing, would gain nothing but to be classed among those very unpopular characters who affect to be better than other people. The doctrines have no hold on ordinary believers,—are not a power in their minds. They have an habitual respect for the sound of them, but no feeling which spreads from the words to the things signified, and forces the mind to take them in, and make them conform to the formula. Whenever conduct is concerned, they look round for Mr. A. and B. to direct them how far to go in obeying Christ."—J. S. Mill, *On Liberty*, p. 24.

All this is indeed indisputable, as against the inconsistencies of Christians; but it is beside the question of the excellence or faultiness of Christian morality.

NOTE F.

See Lecture VIII., p. 99.

It is to be noted throughout these Lectures, in regard to the character and influence of motives in morality, that a motive, whether selfish or unselfish, may be real and efficacious, without any consciousness of it or direct reference to it in each particular instance. Indeed, it is a healthier habit, morally and physically, as a rule, to act rightly and yet unconsciously.

By the same Author.

FAITH AND PHILOSOPHY. Essays on some Tendencies of the Day. 7*s.* 6*d.* (Longmans.)

FRA ANGELICO and other short Poems. 4*s.* 6*d.* (Longmans.)

LIFE OF OUR BLESSED SAVIOUR. From the latest Harmonies. With Introduction and Notes. Second Edition. 2s. (Rivingtons.)

THE SILVER BELLS: an Allegory. Second Edition. 1*s.* (S.P.C.K.)

BOOKS
PUBLISHED
BY JAMES PARKER AND CO.
OXFORD, AND 377, STRAND, LONDON.

Theological, &c.

S. IRENÆUS.
THE WORKS OF S. IRENÆUS, Translated by the late Rev. JOHN KEBLE (forming vol. 42 of the Series of the Library of the Fathers). 8vo., cloth, price to Subscribers, 10s. 6d.

S. AUGUSTINE.
BIBLIOTHECA PATRUM, Vol. I.—S. AURELII AUGUSTINI CONFESSIONES, Post Editionem Parisiensem novissimam ad fidem Codicum Oxoniensium recognitæ, et post Editionem M. DUBOIS, ex ipso Augustino illustratæ. *Editio Secunda.* 8vo., cloth, price to subscribers, 7s.

SERVICE-BOOK OF THE CHURCH OF ENGLAND.
THE SERVICE-BOOK OF THE CHURCH OF ENGLAND, being a New Edition of the "Daily Services of the United Church of England and Ireland," arranged according to the New Table of Lessons. Crown 8vo., roan, 12s.; calf antique or calf limp, 16s.; limp morocco or best morocco, 18s.

REV. JOHN W. BURGON, B.D.
THE LAST TWELVE VERSES OF THE GOSPEL ACCORDING TO S. MARK Vindicated against Recent Critical Objectors and Established, by JOHN W. BURGON, B.D., Vicar of S. Mary-the-Virgin's, Fellow of Oriel College, and Gresham Lecturer in Divinity. With Facsimiles of Codex ℵ and Codex L. 8vo., cloth, 12s.

A PLAIN COMMENTARY ON THE FOUR HOLY GOSPELS, intended chiefly for Devotional Reading. 5 vols., Fcap. 8vo., cloth, £1 1s.

SHORT SERMONS (NINETY-ONE) FOR FAMILY READING: following the Course of the Christian Seasons. Second Series. By the Rev. J. W. BURGON, M.A., Fellow of Oriel, and Vicar of St. Mary's. 2 vols., Fcap., cl., 8s.

The First Series (Ninety) may also be had in Two Volumes, cloth, 8s.

REV. DR. IRONS.
CHRISTIANITY AS TAUGHT BY S. PAUL. The Bampton Lectures for 1870. By WILLIAM J. IRONS, D.D., Prebendary of S. Paul's, London; and Rector of Wadingham, Lincolnshire. To which is added an Appendix of the Continuous Sense of S. Paul's Epistles; with Notes and Metalegomena. 8vo., with Map, cloth, 14s.

THE LORD BISHOP OF WINCHESTER.
ADDRESSES TO THE CANDIDATES FOR ORDINATION ON THE QUESTIONS IN THE ORDINATION SERVICE. By SAMUEL, LORD BISHOP OF OXFORD, Chancellor of the Most Noble Order of the Garter, and Lord High Almoner to Her Majesty the Queen. *Fifth Thousand.* Crown 8vo., cloth, 6s.

SERMONS PREACHED BEFORE THE UNIVERSITY OF OXFORD: Second Series, from 1847 to 1862. By SAMUEL, LORD BISHOP OF OXFORD, Lord High Almoner to the Queen, and Chancellor of the Most Noble Order of the Garter. 8vo., cloth, 10s. 6d.

―――――― Third Series, 1863 to 1870. By SAMUEL, LORD BISHOP OF WINCHESTER, Prelate of the Most Noble Order of the Garter. 8vo., cloth, 7s. 6d.

JOANA J. GRESWELL.
GRAMMATICAL ANALYSIS OF THE HEBREW PSALTER. By JOANA JULIA GRESWELL. Post 8vo., cloth, 6s.

REV. E. B. PUSEY, D.D.

SERMONS preached before the UNIVERSITY OF OXFORD between A.D. 1859 and 1872. By the Rev. E. B. Pusey, D.D., Regius Professor of Hebrew, and Canon of Christ Church. 8vo., cloth, 6s.

THE CHURCH OF ENGLAND A PORTION OF CHRIST'S ONE HOLY CATHOLIC CHURCH, AND A MEANS OF RESTORING VISIBLE UNITY. AN EIRENICON (Part I.), in a Letter to the Author of "The Christian Year." By E. B. Pusey, D.D., Regius Professor of Hebrew, and Canon of Christ Church. *Sixth Thousand.* 8vo., cloth, 7s. 6d.

FIRST LETTER to the Very Rev. J. H. NEWMAN, D.D., in explanation chiefly in regard to the Reverential Love due to the ever-blessed Theotokos, and the Doctrine of her "Immaculate Conception;" with an Analysis of Cardinal de Turrecremata's work on the "Immaculate Conception." (Eirenicon. Part II.) By E. B. Pusey, D.D. 8vo., cloth, 7s. 6d.

IS HEALTHFUL RE-UNION IMPOSSIBLE? (EIRENICON. Part III.) By the Rev. E. B. Pusey, D.D. 8vo., sewed, 6s.

TRACTATUS DE VERITATE CONCEPTIONIS BEATISSIMÆ VIRGINIS, pro Facienda Relatione coram Patribus Concilii Basileæ, Anno Domini MCCCCXXXVII., Mense Julio. Compilatus per Reverendum Patrem, Fratrem Joannem De Turrecremata, S.T.P., &c. Small 4to. (850 pp.), cloth, 12s.

ELEVEN ADDRESSES DURING A RETREAT OF THE COMPANIONS OF THE LOVE OF JESUS, engaged in Perpetual Intercession for the Conversion of Sinners. By the Rev. E. B. Pusey, D.D., &c. 8vo., cloth, 3s. 6d.

DANIEL THE PROPHET. Nine Lectures delivered in the Divinity School of the University of Oxford. With a new Preface. By E. B. Pusey, D.D., &c. *Third Edition. Fifth Thousand.* 8vo., cloth, 10s. 6d.

THE MINOR PROPHETS; with a Commentary Explanatory and Practical, and Introductions to the Several Books. By E. B. Pusey, D.D., &c. 4to., sewed. 5s. each part.

Part I. contains Hosea—Joel, Introduction. | Part IV. Micah i. 13 to Nahum, end.
Part II. Joel, Introduction—Amos vi. 6. | Part V. Habakkuk, Zephaniah, Haggai.
Part III. Amos vi. 6 to Micah i. 12. | [*In preparation.*

P. E. PUSEY, M.A.

THE THREE EPISTLES (ad Nestorium, ii., iii., et ad Joan Antioch) OF ST. CYRIL, ARCHBISHOP OF ALEXANDRIA. A Revised Text, with an old Latin Version and an English Translation. Edited by P. E. Pusey, M.A. 8vo., in wrapper, 3s.

To Subscribers only, 10 vols., 8vo., cloth, 12s. per volume.

A NEW EDITION OF THE WORKS OF S. CYRIL, ARCHBISHOP OF ALEXANDRIA. Edited by P. E. Pusey, M.A. Vols. I. and II., containing the Commentaries upon the Twelve Minor Prophets, and Vol. III., containing the first part of the Commentary on S. John, can be delivered to Subscribers now; Vol. IV., containing a continuation of the latter Book, will be issued in July, 1873. The remaining volumes will be published in due course.

Subscribers' names should be sent to James Parker and Co., Broad-street, Oxford, of whom prospectuses may be obtained.

REV. I. GREGORY SMITH, M.A.

CHARACTERISTICS OF CHRISTIAN MORALITY. Considered in Eight Lectures preached before the University of Oxford, in the year 1873, on the Foundation of the late Rev. John Bampton, M.A., Canon of Salisbury. By the Rev. I. Gregory Smith, M.A., late Fellow of Brasenose College; Vicar of Malvern; and Prebendary of Hereford. [*In the Press.*

REV. WILLIAM BRIGHT, D.D.

A HISTORY OF THE CHURCH, from the EDICT of MILAN, A.D. 313, to the COUNCIL of CHALCEDON, A.D. 451. By WILLIAM BRIGHT, D.D., Regius Professor of Ecclesiastical History and Canon of Christ Church, Oxford. *Second Edition.* Post 8vo., price 10s. 6d.

ANCIENT COLLECTS and OTHER PRAYERS, Selected for Devotional Use from various Rituals, with an Appendix on the Collects in the Prayer-book. By WILLIAM BRIGHT, D.D. *Fourth Edition.* Antique cloth, 5s.

THE LORD BISHOP OF BRECHIN.

AN EXPLANATION OF THE THIRTY-NINE ARTICLES. With an Epistle Dedicatory to the Rev. E. B. PUSEY, D.D. By A. P. FORBES, D.C.L., Bishop of Brechin. Second Edition, Crown 8vo., cloth, 12s.

A SHORT EXPLANATION OF THE NICENE CREED, for the Use of Persons beginning the Study of Theology. By ALEXANDER PENROSE FORBES, D.C.L., Bishop of Brechin. *Second Edition.* Crown 8vo., cloth, 6s.

THE LORD BISHOP OF SALISBURY.

THE BAMPTON LECTURES FOR 1868. THE ADMINISTRATION OF THE HOLY SPIRIT IN THE BODY OF CHRIST. By GEORGE MOBERLY, D.C.L., Lord Bishop of Salisbury. *2nd Edit.* Crown 8vo., cloth, 7s. 6d.

SERMONS ON THE BEATITUDES, with others mostly preached before the University of Oxford. By GEORGE MOBERLY, D.C.L. *Third Edition.* Crown 8vo., cloth, 7s. 6d.

REV. CANON JENKINS.

THE AGE OF THE MARTYRS; or, the First Three Centuries of the Work of the Church of our Lord and Saviour Jesus Christ. By the Rev. J. D. JENKINS, B.D., Canon of Pieter Maritzburg; Fellow of Jesus College, Oxford. Crown 8vo., cloth, 6s.

T. J. BAILEY, B.A.

ORDINUM SACRORUM IN ECCLESIA ANGLICANA DEFENSIO, unacum Statutis, Documentis, et Testimoniis ordinum Anglicanorum valorem probantibus; et Registro Consecrationis Archiepiscopi Parkeri, in Bibliotheca Lambethæ Asservato, Photozincographice expresso. Editore T. J. BAILEY, B.A., e Coll. C. C. Cantab. Ecclesiæ Anglicanæ Sacerdote. Large Folio, cloth, £1 10s.

A DEFENCE OF HOLY ORDERS IN THE CHURCH OF ENGLAND, including the Statutes, Documents, and other Evidence attesting the Validity of Anglican Orders. Edited by the Rev. T. J. BAILEY, B.A., C.C. Coll., Cambridge. Crown 8vo., cloth, 6s.

ARCHDEACON FREEMAN.

THE PRINCIPLES OF DIVINE SERVICE; or, An Inquiry concerning the True Manner of Understanding and Using the Order for Morning and Evening Prayer, and for the Administration of the Holy Communion in the English Church. By the Ven. ARCHDEACON FREEMAN, M.A., Vicar of Thorverton, and Prebendary of Exeter. *A New Edition.* 2 vols., 8vo., cloth, 16s.

CATENA AUREA.

CATENA AUREA. A Commentary on the Four Gospels, collected out of the Works of the Fathers by S. THOMAS AQUINAS. Uniform with the Library of the Fathers. Re-issue. Complete in 6 vols. 8vo., cloth, £2 2s.

T. W. BELCHER, M.D.

OUR LORD'S MIRACLES OF HEALING Considered in relation to some Modern Objections and to Medical Science. By T. W. BELCHER, M.D., M.A., Master in Surgery, Trinity College, Dublin; Fellow of the Royal College of Physicians of Ireland. With Preface by the Most Reverend RICHARD CHENEVIX TRENCH, D.D., Lord Archbishop of Dublin. Crown 8vo., cl., 2s. 6d.

THEOLOGICAL WORKS, &c. (continued).

TEXT-BOOKS FOR OXFORD EXAMINATIONS UNDER THE NEW THEOLOGICAL STATUTE.

THE DEFINITIONS OF THE CATHOLIC FAITH AND CANONS OF DISCIPLINE OF THE FIRST FOUR GENERAL COUNCILS OF THE UNIVERSAL CHURCH. In Greek and English. 2nd Edition. Fcap. 8vo., cloth, 2s. 6d.

DE FIDE ET SYMBOLO: Documenta quædam nec non Aliquorum SS. Patrum Tractatus. Edidit CAROLUS A. HEURTLEY, S.T.P., Dom. Margaretæ Prælector, et Ædis Christi Canonicus. Fcap. 8vo., cloth, 4s. 6d.

S. AURELIUS AUGUSTINUS, Episcopus Hipponensis, de Catechizandis Rudibus, de Fide Rerum quæ non videntur, de Utilitate Credendi. In Usum Juniorum. Edidit C. MARRIOTT, S.T.B., Olim Coll. Oriel. Socius. *New Edition.* Fcap. 8vo., cloth, 3s. 6d.

BEDE'S ECCLESIASTICAL HISTORY OF THE ENGLISH NATION. A New Translation by the Rev. L. GIDLEY, M.A., Chaplain of St. Nicholas', Salisbury. Crown 8vo., cloth, 6s.

A CRITICAL HISTORY OF THE ATHANASIAN CREED, by the Rev. DANIEL WATERLAND, D.D. Edited by the Rev. J. R. KING, M.A. Fcap. 8vo., cloth, 5s.

ANALECTA CHRISTIANA, In usum Tironum. Excerpta, Epistolæ, &c., ex EUSEBII, &c.; S. IGNATII Epistolæ ad Smyrnæos et ad Polycarpum; E. S. CLEMENTIS ALEXANDRI Pædagogo excerpta; S. ATHANASII Sermo contra Gentes. Edidit et Annotationibus illustravit C. MARRIOTT, S.T.B. 8vo., 10s. 6d.

S. CYRIL, ARCHBISHOP OF ALEXANDRIA. THE THREE EPISTLES. Edited by P. E. PUSEY, M.A. (See p. 2.)

DEFENSIO FIDEI NICÆNÆ. A Defence of the Nicene Creed out of the extant writings of the Catholic Doctors who flourished during the three first centuries of the Christian Church. By GEORGE BULL, D.D., Lord Bishop of St. David's. A new Translation. 2 vols., 8vo., 10s.

OXFORD SERIES OF DEVOTIONAL WORKS. Fcap. 8vo.

The Imitation of Christ.
FOUR BOOKS. By Thomas A KEMPIS. Cloth, 4s.

Andrewes' Devotions.
DEVOTIONS. By the Right Rev. Father in God, LAUNCELOT ANDREWES. Translated from the Greek and Latin, and arranged anew. Antique cloth, 5s.

Taylor's Holy Living.
THE RULE AND EXERCISES OF HOLY LIVING. By BISHOP JEREMY TAYLOR. Antique cloth, 4s.

Taylor's Holy Dying.
THE RULE AND EXERCISES OF HOLY DYING. By BISHOP JEREMY TAYLOR. Antique cloth, 4s.

Taylor's Golden Grove.
THE GOLDEN GROVE; a Choice Manual, containing what is to be Believed, Practised, and Desired, or Prayed for. By BISHOP JEREMY TAYLOR. Printed uniform with "Holy Living and Holy Dying." Antique cloth, 3s. 6d.

Sutton's Meditations.
GODLY MEDITATIONS UPON THE MOST HOLY SACRAMENT OF THE LORD'S SUPPER. By CHRISTOPHER SUTTON, D.D., late Prebend of Westminster. A new Edition. Antique cloth, 5s.

Wilson's Sacra Privata.
THE PRIVATE MEDITATIONS, DEVOTIONS, and PRAYERS of the Right Rev. T. WILSON, D.D., Lord Bishop of Sodor and Man. Now first printed entire. Cloth, 4s.

Laud's Devotions.
THE PRIVATE DEVOTIONS of DR. WILLIAM LAUD, Archbishop of Canterbury, and Martyr. Antique cloth, 5s.

Spinckes' Devotions.
TRUE CHURCH OF ENGLAND MAN'S COMPANION IN THE CLOSET; or, a complete Manual of Private Devotions, collected from the Writings of eminent Divines of the Church of England. Floriated borders, antique cloth, 4s.

Ancient Collects.
ANCIENT COLLECTS AND OTHER PRAYERS. Selected for Devotional use from various Rituals. By WM. BRIGHT, D.D. Antique cloth, 5s.

Devout Communicant.
THE DEVOUT COMMUNICANT, exemplified in his Behaviour before, at, and after the Sacrament of the Lord's Supper: Practically suited to all the Parts of that Solemn Ordinance. 7th Edition, revised. Fcap. 8vo., toned paper, red lines, cloth, 4s.

ΕΙΚΩΝ ΒΑΣΙΛΙΚΗ.
THE PORTRAITURE OF HIS SACRED MAJESTY KING CHARLES I. in his Solitudes and Sufferings. Ant. cloth, 5s.

DEVOTIONAL.

THE EVERY-DAY COMPANION. By the Rev. W. H. RIDLEY, M.A., Rector of Hambleden, Bucks. PT. I. Fcap. 8vo., cloth, 2s. PT. II. 1s. 6d. Or in One Volume, cloth, 3s.

THE LIFE OF JESUS CHRIST IN GLORY: Daily Meditations, from Easter Day to the Wednesday after Trinity Sunday. By NOUET. Translated from the French, and adapted to the Use of the English Church. *Third Thousand.* 12mo., cloth, 6s.

A GUIDE FOR PASSING ADVENT HOLILY. By AVRILLON. Translated from the French, and adapted to the use of the English Church. *New Edition.* Fcap. 8vo., cloth, 5s.

ADVENT READINGS FROM THE FATHERS. Fcap. 8vo., cloth, 3s. 6d.

A GUIDE FOR PASSING LENT HOLILY. By AVRILLON. Translated from the French, and adapted to the use of the English Church. Fourth Edition. Fcap. 8vo., cloth, 6s.

LENT READINGS FROM THE FATHERS. *A New Edition.* Fcap. 8vo., cloth, 5s.

MEDITATIONS FOR THE FORTY DAYS OF LENT. With a Prefatory Notice by the ARCHBISHOP OF DUBLIN. 18mo., cloth, 2s. 6d.

OF THE IMITATION OF CHRIST. FOUR BOOKS. By THOMAS A KEMPIS. A New Edition revised. On toned paper, with red border-lines, &c. Small 4to., cloth, 12s. Also, printed in red and black, with red lines, on toned paper. Fcap., cloth, 4s.

THE INNER LIFE. HYMNS on the "Imitation of Christ," by THOMAS A'KEMPIS; designed especially for Use at Holy Communion. By the Author of "Thoughts from a Girl's Life," "Light at Eventide," &c. Fcap. 8vo., cloth, 3s.

DAILY STEPS TOWARDS HEAVEN; or, Practical Thoughts on the Gospel History, for every day in the year. With Titles and Characters of Christ. *Sixteenth Edition.* 32mo., roan, 2s. 6d.; morocco, 4s. 6d.

——————— LARGE-TYPE EDITION, sq. cr. 8vo., cloth, 5s.

FORM OF PRAISE AND PRAYER IN THE MANNER OF OFFICES. Edited by the Hon. and Rev. W. H. LYTTELTON, M.A. Cr. 8vo., 3s. 6d.

THOUGHTS DURING SICKNESS. By ROBERT BRETT, Author of "The Doctrine of the Cross," &c. Fcap. 8vo., limp cloth, 1s. 6d.

THE PASTOR IN HIS CLOSET; or, A Help to the Devotions of the Clergy. By JOHN ARMSTRONG, D.D., late Lord Bishop of Grahamstown. *Third Edition.* Fcap. 8vo., cloth, 2s.

THE CROSS OF CHRIST; or, Meditations on the Death and Passion of our Blessed Lord and Saviour. Edited by W. F. HOOK, D.D., Dean of Chichester. Crown 8vo., cloth, 3s. 6d.

SERMONS, &c.

PAROCHIAL SERMONS. By E. B. PUSEY, D.D. Vol. I. From Advent to Whitsuntide. *Seventh Edition.* 8vo., cloth, 6s. Vol. II. *Sixth Edition.* 8vo., cloth, 6s.

NINE SERMONS PREACHED BEFORE THE UNIVERSITY OF OXFORD. By E. B. PUSEY, D.D., and printed between 1843—1855. In one volume. 8vo., cloth. [*Reprinting.*

PAROCHIAL SERMONS PREACHED AND PRINTED ON VARIOUS OCCASIONS, 1832—1850. By E. B. PUSEY, D.D. In one volume. 8vo., cloth, 6s.

ILLUSTRATIONS OF FAITH. EIGHT PLAIN SERMONS, by a Writer in the "Tracts for the Christian Seasons" [the late Rev. EDWARD MONRO]:—Abel; Enoch; Noah; Abraham; Isaac, Jacob, and Joseph; Moses; The Walls of Jericho; Conclusions. Fcap. 8vo., cloth, 2s. 6d.

Uniform, and by the same Author,

PLAIN SERMONS ON THE BOOK OF COMMON PRAYER. Fcap. 8vo., cloth, 5s.

HISTORICAL AND PRACTICAL SERMONS ON THE SUFFERINGS AND RESURRECTION OF OUR LORD. 2 vols., Fcap. 8vo., cloth, 10s.

SERMONS ON NEW TESTAMENT CHARACTERS. Fcap. 8vo., 4s.

CHRISTIAN SEASONS.—Short and Plain Sermons for every Sunday and Holyday throughout the Year. Edited by the late Bishop of Grahamstown. 4 vols., Fcap. 8vo., cloth, 16s.

——————————— A Second Series of Sermons for the Christian Seasons. Uniform with the above. 4 vols., Fcap. 8vo., cloth, 16s.

ARMSTRONG'S PAROCHIAL SERMONS. Parochial Sermons, by JOHN ARMSTRONG, D.D., late Lord Bishop of Grahamstown. Fcap. 8vo., cl., 5s.

ARMSTRONG'S SERMONS FOR FASTS AND FESTIVALS. A new Edition. Fcap. 8vo., 5s.

SHORT ALLEGORICAL SERMONS. CONTENTS: 1. The City of the Lost; 2. The Prisoner of Hope; 3. The Soldier; 4. The Hounds; 5. The Slaves; 6. The Stone of Separation; 7. The Stranger; 8. The Exile; 9. The Unnatural Sentence; 10. The Guest-chamber; 11. The Three Fields; 12. The Bargain. Fcap. 8vo., toned paper, cloth, 3s.

PERSONAL RESPONSIBILITY OF MAN; AND THE PROPHETS OF THE LORD—THEIR MESSAGE TO THEIR OWN AGE AND TO OURS. Sermons preached during the SEASON OF LENT, 1868 and 1869, in Oxford. With a Preface by the BISHOP OF OXFORD. 2 vols. 8vo., 12s. 6d.

SERMONS PREACHED DURING THE SEASONS OF LENT, 1870 and 1871, in Oxford. 8vo., cloth. [*Nearly ready.*

SERMONS FOR THE HOLY SEASONS OF THE CHURCH. Advent to Trinity. By GEORGE HUNTINGTON, M.A., Rector of Tenby, and Domestic Chaplain to the Right Hon. the Earl of Crawford and Balcarres. *Second Edition.* Crown 8vo., cloth, 5s.

SERMONS ON SOME SUBJECTS OF RECENT CONTROVERSY preached before the UNIVERSITY OF OXFORD. By CHARLES A. HEURTLEY, D.D., Margaret Professor of Divinity, and Canon of Christ Church. 8vo., cloth, 5s.

SERMONS ON THE OFFICES FOR THE VISITATION OF THE SICK AND THE BURIAL OF THE DEAD. By CHARLES JAMES BURTON, M.A., Chancellor of Carlisle, and Vicar of Lydd. Post 8vo., cloth, 3s. 6d.

Works of the Standard English Divines,

PUBLISHED IN THE LIBRARY OF ANGLO-CATHOLIC THEOLOGY,

AT THE FOLLOWING PRICES IN CLOTH.

ANDREWES' (BP.) COMPLETE WORKS. 11 vols., 8vo., £3 7s.
    THE SERMONS. (Separate.) 5 vols., £1 15s.

BEVERIDGE'S (BP.) COMPLETE WORKS. 12 vols., 8vo., £4 4s.
    THE ENGLISH THEOLOGICAL WORKS. 10 vols., £3 10s.

BRAMHALL'S (ABP.) WORKS, WITH LIFE AND LETTERS, &c. 5 vols., 8vo., £1 15s. (Vol. 2 cannot be sold separately.)

BULL'S (BP.) HARMONY ON JUSTIFICATION. 2 vols., 8vo., 10s.
——————— DEFENCE OF THE NICENE CREED. 2 vols., 10s.
——————— JUDGMENT OF THE CATHOLIC CHURCH. 5s.

COSIN'S (BP.) WORKS COMPLETE. 5 vols., 8vo., £1 10s. (Vol. 1 cannot be sold separately.)

CRAKANTHORP'S DEFENSIO ECCLESIÆ ANGLICANÆ. 8vo., 7s.

FRANK'S SERMONS. 2 vols., 8vo., 10s.

FORBES' CONSIDERATIONES MODESTÆ. 2 vols., 8vo., 12s.

GUNNING'S PASCHAL, OR LENT FAST. 8vo., 6s.

HAMMOND'S PRACTICAL CATECHISM. 8vo., 5s.
——————— MISCELLANEOUS THEOLOGICAL WORKS. 5s.
——————— THIRTY-ONE SERMONS. 2 Parts. 10s.

HICKES'S TWO TREATISES ON THE CHRISTIAN PRIESTHOOD. 3 vols., 8vo., 15s.

JOHNSON'S (JOHN) THEOLOGICAL WORKS. 2 vols., 8vo., 10s.
——————— ENGLISH CANONS. 2 vols., 12s.

LAUD'S (ABP.) COMPLETE WORKS. 7 vols., (9 Parts,) 8vo., £2 17s.

L'ESTRANGE'S ALLIANCE OF DIVINE OFFICES. 8vo., 6s.

MARSHALL'S PENITENTIAL DISCIPLINE. (This volume cannot be sold separate from the complete set.)

NICHOLSON'S (BP.) EXPOSITION OF THE CATECHISM. (This volume cannot be sold separate from the complete set.)

OVERALL'S (BP.) CONVOCATION-BOOK OF 1606. 8vo., 5s.

PEARSON'S (BP.) VINDICIÆ EPISTOLARUM S. IGNATII. 2 vols. 8vo., 10s.

THORNDIKE'S (HERBERT) THEOLOGICAL WORKS COMPLETE. 6 vols., (10 Parts,) 8vo., £2 10s.

WILSON'S (BP.) WORKS COMPLETE. With LIFE, by Rev. J. KEBLE. 7 vols., (8 Parts,) 8vo., £3 3s.

A complete set, £25.

THE AUTHORIZED EDITIONS OF
THE CHRISTIAN YEAR,
With the Author's latest Corrections and Additions.

Small 4to. Edition.

Handsomely printed on toned paper, with red border lines and initial letters.

	£	s.	d.
Cloth extra	0	10	6
Calf antique	1	0	0
Morocco antique	1	8	0

Foolscap 8vo. Edition.

	s.	d.
Cloth	3	6
Morocco, plain	8	0
Morocco, best plain	10	6
Morocco antique	14	0
Calf antique	10	0
Vellum	10	0

24mo. Edition.

	s.	d.
Cloth	2	0
Morocco, plain	6	0
Morocco, best plain	7	6
Morocco antique	10	0
Calf antique	8	0
Vellum	8	0

32mo. Edition.

	s.	d.
Cloth, limp	1	0
Cloth boards, gilt edges	1	6
Morocco, plain	3	0
Morocco, best plain	7	0
Morocco antique	8	0
Calf antique	6	6
Vellum	6	6

48mo. Edition.

	s.	d.
Cloth, limp	0	6
Cloth boards	0	9
Roan	1	6

Facsimile of the 1st Edition, with a list of the variations from the Original Text which the Author made in later Editions. 2 vols., 12mo., boards . . 7s. 6d.

AN ILLUSTRATED EDITION will shortly be issued under the direction of the Author's Representatives.

NOTICE.—Messrs. Parker are the sole Publishers of the Editions of the "Christian Year" issued with the sanction and under the direction of the Author's representatives. All Editions without their imprint are unauthorized.

By the same Author.

LYRA INNOCENTIUM. Thoughts in Verse on Christian Children. *Twelfth Edition.* Fcap. 8vo., cloth, 5s.

———— 48mo. edition, limp cloth, 6d.; cloth boards, 1s.

MISCELLANEOUS POEMS BY THE REV. JOHN KEBLE, M.A., Vicar of Hursley. [With Preface by G. M.] *Third Edition.* Fcap., cloth, 6s.

THE PSALTER, OR PSALMS OF DAVID: In English Verse. *Fourth Edition.* Fcap. cloth, 6s.

The above may also be had in various bindings.

A CONCORDANCE TO THE "CHRISTIAN YEAR." Fcap. 8vo., toned paper, cloth, 7s. 6d.

MUSINGS ON THE "CHRISTIAN YEAR;" with GLEANINGS from Thirty Years' Intercourse with the late Rev. J. Keble, by CHARLOTTE M. YONGE: to which are added Recollections of Hursley, by FRANCES M. WILBRAHAM. *Second Edition.* Fcap. 8vo., cloth, 7s. 6d.

MEMOIR OF THE REV. J. KEBLE, M.A. By Sir J. T. Coleridge. *Third Edition.* Post 8vo., cloth, 10s. 6d.

Church Poetry.

WORKS BY THE LATE ISAAC WILLIAMS.

THE CATHEDRAL; or, The Catholic and Apostolic Church in England. *Eighth Edition.* Fcap. 8vo., 7s. 6d.

——————— *Seventh Edition.* 32mo., 4s. 6d.

THOUGHTS IN PAST YEARS. *Sixth Edition.* 32mo., 4s. 6d.

THE BAPTISTERY, OR THE WAY OF ETERNAL LIFE. With Plates from BOETIUS A BOLSWERT. New Edition. 2 vols., Fcap. 8vo., cloth, 14s.

——————— *A New Edition.* 32mo., cl., 3s. 6d.

THE CHRISTIAN SCHOLAR. Fcap. 8vo., 10s. 6d.

——————— *A New Edition.* 32mo., 4s. 6d.

THE SEVEN DAYS; or, The Old and New Creation. *Second Edition*, Fcap. 8vo., 7s. 6d.

THE CHILD'S CHRISTIAN YEAR.

THE CHILD'S CHRISTIAN YEAR. Hymns for every Sunday and Holyday throughout the Year. *Cheap Edition*, 18mo., cloth, 1s.

BISHOP CLEVELAND COXE.

COXE'S CHRISTIAN BALLADS. Foolscap 8vo., cloth, 3s. Also selected Poems in a packet, 32mo., sewed, 1s.

Parochial.

THE CONFIRMATION CLASS-BOOK: Notes for Lessons, with APPENDIX, containing Questions and Summaries for the Use of the Candidates. By E. M. HOLMES, LL.B., Rector of Marsh Gibbon, Bucks; Diocesan Inspector of Schools; Author of the "Catechist's Manual." Fcap. 8vo., limp cloth, 2s. 6d.

Also, in wrapper, THE QUESTIONS AND SUMMARIES separate, 4 sets of 128 pp. in packets, 1s. each.

THE CATECHIST'S MANUAL; with an Introduction by SAMUEL, LORD BISHOP OF OXFORD. *Fifth Thousand.* Crown 8vo., limp cloth, 5s.

SHORT NOTES OF SEVEN YEARS' WORK IN A COUNTRY PARISH. By R. F. WILSON, M.A., Vicar of Rownhams, Prebendary of Sarum, and Examining Chaplain to the Bishop of Salisbury. Fcap. 8vo., cloth, 4s.

THE CHURCH AND THE SCHOOL; or, Hints on Clerical Life. By HENRY WALFORD BELLAIRS, M.A., one of Her Majesty's Inspectors of Schools. Crown 8vo., cloth, 5s.

THE CHURCH'S WORK IN OUR LARGE TOWNS. By GEORGE HUNTINGTON, M.A., Rector of Tenby, and Domestic Chaplain of the Rt. Hon. the Earl of Crawford and Balcarres. Second Edition, revised and enlarged, Crown 8vo., cloth, 6s.

BREVIATES FROM HOLY SCRIPTURE, arranged for use by the Bed of Sickness. By the Rev. G. ARDEN, M.A., Rector of Winterborne-Came; Domestic Chaplain to the Right Hon. the Earl of Devon. *2nd Ed.* Fcap. 8vo., 2s.

THE CURE OF SOULS. By the Rev. G. ARDEN, M.A., Rector of Winterborne-Came, and Author of "Breviates from Holy Scripture," &c. Fcap. 8vo., cloth, 2s. 6d.

THE ELEMENTS OF PSYCHOLOGY.

THE ELEMENTS OF PSYCHOLOGY, ON THE PRINCIPLES OF BENEKE, Stated and Illustrated in a Simple and Popular Manner by DR. G. RAUE, Professor in the Medical College, Philadelphia; Fourth Edition, considerably Altered, Improved, and Enlarged, by JOHANN GOTTLIEB DRESSLER, late Director of the Normal School at Bautzen. Translated from the German. Post 8vo., cloth, 6s.

REV. CANON GREGORY.

ARE WE BETTER THAN OUR FATHERS? or, A Comparative View of the Social Position of England at the Revolution of 1688, and at the Present Time. FOUR LECTURES delivered in St. Paul's Cathedral in November, 1871. By ROBERT GREGORY, M.A., Canon of St. Paul's. Crown 8vo., 2s. 6d.

REV. L. BIGGE-WITHER.

A NEARLY LITERAL TRANSLATION OF HOMER'S ODYSSEY into ACCENTUATED DRAMATIC VERSE. By the Rev. LOVELACE BIGGE-WITHER, M.A. Large fcap. 8vo., toned paper, cloth, 10s. 6d.

PROFESSOR BONAMY PRICE.

THE PRINCIPLES OF CURRENCY: Six Lectures delivered at Oxford. By BONAMY PRICE, Professor of Political Economy in the University of Oxford. With a Letter from M. MICHEL CHEVALIER, on the History of the Treaty of Commerce with France. 8vo., cloth, 7s. 6d.

REV. T. CHILDE BARKER.

ARYAN CIVILIZATION, its Religious Origin and its Progress, with an Account of the Religion, Laws, and Institutions of Greece and Rome, based on the work of DE COULANGES. By the Rev. T. CHILDE BARKER, Vicar of Spelsbury, Oxfordshire, and late Student of Christ Church. Crown 8vo., cl., 5s.

PROFESSOR DAUBENY.

MISCELLANIES: BEING A COLLECTION OF MEMOIRS and ESSAYS ON SCIENTIFIC AND LITERARY SUBJECTS, published at Various Times, by the late CHARLES DAUBENY, M.D., F.R.S., Professor of Botany in the University of Oxford, &c. 2 vols., 8vo., cloth, 21s.

FUGITIVE POEMS, relating to Subjects connected with Natural History and Physical Science, Archæology, &c. Selected by the late CHARLES DAUBENY, &c. Fcap. 8vo., cl., 5s.

PROFESSOR GOLDWIN SMITH.

THE REORGANIZATION OF THE UNIVERSITY OF OXFORD. By GOLDWIN SMITH. Post 8vo., limp cloth, 2s.

LECTURES ON THE STUDY OF HISTORY, DELIVERED IN OXFORD, 1859—61. Second Edition. Crown 8vo., limp cloth, 3s. 6d.

IRISH HISTORY AND IRISH CHARACTER. Second Edition. Post 8vo., 5s.

———————— Cheap Edition, Fcap. 8vo., sewed, 1s. 6d.

THE EMPIRE. A SERIES OF LETTERS PUBLISHED IN "THE DAILY NEWS," 1862, 1863. Post 8vo., cloth, price 6s.

W. WILKINSON.

ENGLISH COUNTRY HOUSES. FORTY-FIVE VIEWS AND PLANS of recently erected Mansions, Private Residences, Parsonage-Houses, Farm-Houses, Lodges, and Cottages; with the actual cost of each, and a PRACTICAL TREATISE ON HOUSE-BUILDING. By WILLIAM WILKINSON, Architect, Oxford. Royal 4to., ornamental cloth, £1 16s.

THE PRAYER-BOOK CALENDAR.
THE CALENDAR OF THE PRAYER-BOOK ILLUSTRATED.
(Comprising the first portion of the "Calendar of the Anglican Church," with additional Illustrations, &c.) With Two Hundred Engravings from Medieval Works of Art. *Sixth Thousand.* Fcap. 8vo., cloth, 6s.

THE LATE CHARLES WINSTON.
AN INQUIRY INTO THE DIFFERENCE OF STYLE OBSERVABLE IN ANCIENT GLASS PAINTINGS, especially in England, with Hints on Glass Painting, by the late CHARLES WINSTON. With Corrections and Additions by the Author. 2 vols., Medium 8vo., cloth, £1 11s. 6d.

JOHN EDWIN CUSSANS.
INVENTORY OF FURNITURE AND ORNAMENTS REMAINING IN ALL THE PARISH CHURCHES OF HERTFORDSHIRE in the last year of the Reign of King Edward the Sixth: Transcribed from the Original Records, by JOHN EDWIN CUSSANS, F.R.Hist.S. Cr. 8vo., lp. cl., 4s.

G. G. SCOTT, F.S.A.
GLEANINGS FROM WESTMINSTER ABBEY. By GEORGE GILBERT SCOTT, R.A., F.S.A. With Appendices supplying Further Particulars, and completing the History of the Abbey Buildings, by Several Writers. *Second Edition,* enlarged, containing many new Illustrations by O. Jewitt and others. Medium 8vo., 15s.

REV. SAMUEL LYSONS, F.S.A.
OUR BRITISH ANCESTORS: WHO AND WHAT WERE THEY? An Inquiry serving to elucidate the Traditional History of the Early Britons by means of recent Excavations, Etymology, Remnants of Religious Worship, Inscriptions, Craniology, and Fragmentary Collateral History. By the Rev. SAMUEL LYSONS, M.A., F.S.A., Rector of Rodmarton, and Perpetual Curate of St. Luke's, Gloucester. Post 8vo., cloth, 12s.

M. VIOLLET-LE-DUC.
THE MILITARY ARCHITECTURE OF THE MIDDLE AGES, Translated from the French of M. VIOLLET-LE-DUC. By M. MACDERMOTT, Esq., Architect. With the 151 original French Engravings. Medium 8vo., cloth, £1 1s.

JOHN HEWITT.
ANCIENT ARMOUR AND WEAPONS IN EUROPE. By JOHN HEWITT, Member of the Archæological Institute of Great Britain. Vols. II. and III., comprising the Period from the Fourteenth to the Seventeenth Century, completing the work, 1l. 12s. Also Vol. I., from the Iron Period of the Northern Nations to the end of the Thirteenth Century, 18s. The work complete, 3 vols., 8vo., 2l. 10s.

REV. PROFESSOR STUBBS.
THE TRACT "DE INVENTIONE SANCTÆ CRUCIS NOSTRÆ IN MONTE ACUTO ET DE DUCTIONE EJUSDEM APUD WALTHAM," now first printed from the Manuscript in the British Museum, with Introduction and Notes by WILLIAM STUBBS, M.A., Vicar of Navestock, late Fellow of Trinity College, Oxford. Royal 8vo., uniform with the Works issued by the Master of the Rolls, (only 100 copies printed,) price 5s.; Demy 8vo., 3s. 6d.

HENRY GODWIN, F.S.A.
THE ARCHÆOLOGIST'S HANDBOOK. By HENRY GODWIN, F.S.A. This work contains a summary of the materials which are available for the investigation of the Monuments of this country, arranged chiefly under their several successive periods, from the earliest times to the fifteenth century,—together with Tables of Dates, Kings, &c., Lists of Coins, Cathedrals, Castles, Monasteries, &c. Crown 8vo., cloth, 7s. 6d.

JOHN HENRY PARKER, C.B., F.S.A., HON. M.A. OXON.

THE ARCHÆOLOGY OF ROME. By JOHN HENRY PARKER, C.B., F.S.A., Hon. M.A. Oxon. Medium 8vo. Illustrated by Woodcuts.
[*In the Press.*

AN INTRODUCTION TO THE STUDY OF GOTHIC ARCHITECTURE. *Fourth Edition*, Revised and Enlarged, with 180 Illustrations, and a Glossarial Index. Fcap. 8vo. [*Reprinting.*

A CONCISE GLOSSARY OF TERMS USED IN GRECIAN, ROMAN, ITALIAN, AND GOTHIC ARCHITECTURE. A New Edition, revised. Fcap. 8vo., with 470 Illustrations, in ornamental cloth, 7s. 6d.

THE ARCHITECTURAL ANTIQUITIES OF THE CITY OF WELLS. By JOHN HENRY PARKER, F.S.A., Hon. M.A. Oxon., Honorary Member of the Somerset Archæological Society, &c. Illustrated by Plans and Views. Medium 8vo., cloth, 5s.

ILLUSTRATIONS OF ARCHITECTURAL ANTIQUITIES.

WELLS: 32 Photographs, Folio size, in portfolio, price 3*l*. 3s.; or separately, 2s. 6d. each.

Also 16 Photographs, in 8vo., reduced from the above, in a case, price 15s.; or separately, 1s. each.

GLASTONBURY ABBEY: 9 Photographs, Folio size, in portfolio, price 1*l*.; or separately, 2s. 6d. each.

DORSETSHIRE: 23 Photographs, Folio size, in portfolio, price 4*l*. 4s.; or separately, 2s. 6d. each.

AN ATTEMPT TO DISCRIMINATE THE STYLES OF ARCHITECTURE IN ENGLAND, FROM THE CONQUEST TO THE REFORMATION: WITH A SKETCH OF THE GRECIAN AND ROMAN ORDERS. By the late THOMAS RICKMAN, F.S.A. *Sixth Edition*, with considerable Additions, chiefly Historical, by JOHN HENRY PARKER, F.S.A., Hon. M.A. Oxon., and numerous Illustrations by O. Jewitt. 8vo. [*Reprinting.*

SOME ACCOUNT OF DOMESTIC ARCHITECTURE IN ENGLAND, from Richard II. to Henry VIII. (or the Perpendicular Style). With Numerous Illustrations of Existing Remains from Original Drawings. By the EDITOR OF "THE GLOSSARY OF ARCHITECTURE." In 2 vols., 8vo., 1*l*. 10s.

Also,

FROM EDWARD I. TO RICHARD II. (the Edwardian Period, or the Decorated Style). 8vo., 21s.

THE MEDIÆVAL ARCHITECTURE OF CHESTER. By JOHN HENRY PARKER, F.S.A., Hon. M.A. Oxon. With an Historical Introduction by the Rev. FRANCIS GROSVENOR. Illustrated by Engravings by J. H. Le Keux, O. Jewitt, &c. 8vo., cloth, 5s.

REV. L. M. HUMBERT, M.A.

MEMORIALS OF THE HOSPITAL OF ST. CROSS AND ALMSHOUSE OF NOBLE POVERTY. By the Rev. L. M. HUMBERT, M.A., Master of St. Cross. Illustrated with Thirteen Photographs, by W. SAVAGE, and numerous Woodcuts. 4to., cloth extra, gilt edges, 15s.; morocco elegant, 30s.

H. P. WRIGHT, M.A.

THE STORY OF THE "DOMUS DEI" OF PORTSMOUTH, commonly called the Royal Garrison Church. By H. P. WRIGHT, M.A., Chaplain to the Forces, and Chaplain to H.R.H. the Duke of Cambridge, K.G. Crown 8vo., with Photographic and other Illustrations, cloth, 7s. 6d.

J. T. BLIGHT, F.S.A.

THE CROMLECHS OF CORNWALL: with some Account of other Prehistoric Sepulchral Monuments, and Articles found in connection with them, in the same County. By J. T. BLIGHT, F.S.A. Medium 8vo., with numerous Illustrations. [*In the Press.*

THE NEW SCHOOL-HISTORY OF ENGLAND, from Early Writers and the National Records. By the Author of "The Annals of England." *Fifth Thousand.* Crown 8vo., with Four Maps, limp cloth, 5s.

ANNALS OF ENGLAND. An Epitome of English History. From Cotemporary Writers, the Rolls of Parliament, and other Public Records. 3 vols. Fcap. 8vo., with Illustrations, cloth, 15s. *Recommended by the Examiners in the School of Modern History at Oxford.*
Vol. I. From the Roman Era to the Death of Richard II. Cloth, 5s.
Vol. II. From the Accession of the House of Lancaster to Charles I. Cloth, 5s.
Vol. III. From the Commonwealth to the Death of Queen Anne. Cloth, 5s.
—————————— A New Library Edition, revised and enlarged, with additional Woodcuts. 8vo. [*In the Press.*

JELF'S GREEK GRAMMAR.—A Grammar of the Greek Language, chiefly from the text of Raphael Kühner. By Wm. Edw. Jelf, B.D., late Student and Censor of Ch. Ch. *Fourth Edition, with Additions and Corrections.* 2 vols. 8vo., 1l. 10s.
This Grammar is in general use at Oxford, Cambridge, Dublin, and Durham; at Eton, King's College, London, and most other public schools.

MADVIG'S LATIN GRAMMAR. A Latin Grammar for the Use of Schools. By Professor Madvig, with additions by the Author. Translated by the Rev. G. Woods, M.A. *New Edition, with an Index of Authors.* 8vo., cloth, 12s.
Competent authorities pronounce this work to be the very best Latin Grammar yet published in England. This new Edition contains an Index to the Authors quoted.

THE ETHICS OF ARISTOTLE. With Notes by the Rev. W. E. Jelf, B.D., Author of "A Greek Grammar," &c. 8vo., cloth, 12s.
The Text separately, 5s. The Notes separately, 7s. 6d.

✓ **LAWS OF THE GREEK ACCENTS.** By John Griffiths, M.A. *Fifteenth Edition.* 16mo., price 6d. (*Uniform with Oxford Pocket Classics.*)

TWELVE RUDIMENTARY RULES FOR LATIN PROSE COMPOSITION: with Examples and Exercises, for the use of Beginners. By the Rev. Edward Moore, D.D., Principal of St. Edmund Hall, Oxford, and late Fellow and Tutor of Queen's College. *Second Edition.* 16mo., 6d. (*Uniform with Oxford Pocket Classics.*)

RUDIMENTARY RULES, with Examples, for the Use of Beginners in Greek Prose Composition. By John Mitchinson, D.C.L., Fellow of Pembroke College, Oxford; Head Master of the King's School, and Hon. Canon, Canterbury. 16mo., sewed, 1s. (*Uniform with Oxford Pocket Classics.*)

PRÆLECTIONES ACADEMICÆ IN HOMERUM, Oxonii Habitæ Annis MDCCLXXVI—MDCCLXXXIII. A Joanne Randolph, S.T.P., Poeticæ Publico Prælectore, posteà Episcopo Londinensi. 8vo., cloth, 7s. 6d.

THUCYDIDES, with Notes, chiefly Historical and Geographical. By the late T. Arnold, D.D. With Indices by the Rev. R. P. G. Tiddeman. *Sixth Edition.* 3 vols., 8vo., cloth lettered, £1 16s.

ERASMI COLLOQUIA SELECTA: Arranged for Translation and Re-translation; adapted for the Use of Boys who have begun the Latin Syntax. By Edward C. Lowe, D.D., Head Master of S. John's Middle School, Hurstpierpoint. Fcap. 8vo., strong binding, 3s.

PORTA LATINA: A Selection from Latin Authors, for Translation and Re-Translation; arranged in a Progressive Course, as an Introduction to the Latin Tongue. By Edward C. Lowe, D.D., Head Master of Hurstpierpoint School; Editor of Erasmus' "Colloquies," &c. Fcap. 8vo., strongly bound, 3s.

TRILINEAR CO-ORDINATES. With Examples. Intended chiefly for the Use of Junior Students. By C. J. C. Price, M.A., Fellow and Mathematical Lecturer of Exeter College, Oxford. Post 8vo., cloth, 8s.

A SERIES OF GREEK AND LATIN CLASSICS
FOR THE USE OF SCHOOLS.

GREEK POETS.

	Cloth. s. d.		Cloth. s. d.
Æschylus	3 0	Sophocles	3 0
Aristophanes. 2 vols.	6 0	Homeri Ilias	3 6
Euripides. 3 vols.	6 6	——— Odyssea	3 0
——— Tragœdiæ Sex	3 6		

GREEK PROSE WRITERS.

Aristotelis Ethica	2 0	Thucydides. 2 vols.	5 0
Demosthenes de Corona, et } Æschines in Ctesiphontem }	2 0	Xenophontis Memorabilia	1 4
		——— Anabasis	2 0
Herodotus. 2 vols.	6 0		

LATIN POETS.

Horatius	2 0	Lucretius	2 0
Juvenalis et Persius	1 6	Phædrus	1 4
Lucanus	2 6	Virgilius	2 6

LATIN PROSE WRITERS.

Cæsaris Commentarii, cum Supplementis Auli Hirtii et aliorum	2 6	Ciceronis Tusc. Disp. Lib. V.	2 0
		Ciceronis Orationes Selectæ	3 6
——— Commentarii de Bello Gallico	1 6	Cornelius Nepos	1 4
		Livius. 4 vols.	6 0
Cicero De Officiis, de Senectute, et de Amicitia	2 0	Sallustius	2 0
		Tacitus. 2 vols.	5 0

TEXTS WITH SHORT NOTES.
UNIFORM WITH THE SERIES OF "OXFORD POCKET CLASSICS."

GREEK WRITERS. TEXTS AND NOTES.

SOPHOCLES.

	s. d.		s. d.
Ajax (*Text and Notes*)	1 0	Antigone (*Text and Notes*)	1 0
Electra ,,	1 0	Philoctetes ,,	1 0
Œdipus Rex ,,	1 0	Trachiniæ ,,	1 0
Œdipus Coloneus ,,	1 0		

The Notes only, in one vol., cloth, 3s.

ÆSCHYLUS.

Persæ (*Text and Notes*)	1 0	Choephoræ (*Text and Notes*)	1 0
Prometheus Vinctus ,,	1 0	Eumenides ,,	1 0
Septem Contra Thebas ,,	1 0	Supplices ,,	1 0
Agamemnon ,,	1 0		

The Notes only, in one vol., cloth, 3s. 6d.

ARISTOPHANES.

The Knights (*Text and Notes*)	1 0	Acharnians ,,	1 0
The Birds (*Text and Notes*)	1 6		

EURIPIDES.

		s.	d.			s.	d.
HECUBA (*Text and Notes*)	.	1	0	PHŒNISSÆ (*Text and Notes*)	.	1	0
MEDEA "	. .	1	0	ALCESTIS "	.	1	0
ORESTES "	. .	1	0	The above, Notes only, in one vol., cloth, 3s.			
HIPPOLYTUS "	. .	1	0	BACCHÆ "	.	1	0

HOMERUS . . . . . ILIAS, LIB. I.—VI. (*Text and Notes*) . 2 0

DEMOSTHENES.

DE CORONA (*Text and Notes*) . 2 0 | OLYNTHIAC ORATIONS . . 1 0
PHILIPPIC ORATIONS, *in the Press.*

ÆSCHINES . . . . . IN CTESIPHONTEM (*Text and Notes*) . 2 0

LATIN WRITERS. TEXTS AND NOTES.
VIRGILIUS.

BUCOLICA (*Text and Notes*) . 1 0 | ÆNEIDOS, LIB. I.—III. (*Text*
GEORGICA " . 2 0 | *and Notes*) . . 1 0

HORATIUS.

CARMINA, &c. (*Text and Notes*) 2 0 | EPISTOLÆ ET ARS POETICA (*Text*
SATIRÆ " 1 0 | *and Notes*) . . 1 0
The Notes only, in one vol., cloth, 2s.

PHÆDRUS . . . FABULÆ (*Text and Notes*) 1 0
LIVIUS . . . . LIB. XXI.—XXIV. (*Text and Notes*) sewed, 4s.; cloth, 4 6

SALLUSTIUS.

JUGURTHA (*Text and Notes*) . 1 6 | CATILINA (*Text and Notes*) . 1 0

M. T. CICERO.

		s.	d.
IN Q.CÆCILIUM — DIVINATIO			
(*Text and Notes*) . .	1	0	
IN VERREM ACTIO PRIMA .	1	0	
PRO LEGE MANILIA, et PRO			
ARCHIA	1	0	
IN CATILINAM . . .	1	0	

PRO PLANCIO (*Text and Notes*) . 1 6
PRO MILONE 1 0
ORATIONES PHILIPPICÆ, I., II. 1 6
The above, Notes only, in one vol., cloth, 3s. 6d.
DE SENECTUTE et DE AMICITIA 1 0
EPISTOLÆ SELECTÆ. Pars I. 1 6

CÆSAR . . . . LIB. I.—III. (*Text and Notes*) . . 1 0
CORNELIUS NEPOS. LIVES (*Text and Notes*) . . 1 6
TACITUS. ANNALS. NOTES only, 2 vols., 16mo., cloth . . 7 0

Other portions of several of the above-named Authors are in preparation.

POETARUM SCENICORUM GRÆCORUM, Æschyli, Sophoclis, Euripidis, et Aristophanis, Fabulæ, Superstites, et Perditarum Fragmenta. Ex recognitione GUIL. DINDORFII. Editio Quinta. Royal 8vo., cloth, 21s.

Uniform with the Oxford Pocket Classics.

THE LIVES OF THE MOST EMINENT ENGLISH POETS; WITH CRITICAL OBSERVATIONS ON THEIR WORKS. By SAMUEL JOHNSON. 3 vols., 24mo., cloth, 2s. 6d. each.

CHOICE EXTRACTS FROM MODERN FRENCH AUTHORS, for the use of Schools. 18mo., cloth, 3s.

THE OXFORD UNIVERSITY CALENDAR 1873. Corrected to the end of December, 1872. 12mo., cloth, 4s. 6d.

THE OXFORD TEN-YEAR BOOK: A Complete Register of University Honours and Distinctions, made up to the end of the Year 1870. Crown 8vo., roan, 7s. 6d.

THE OXFORD UNIVERSITY EXAMINATION PAPERS, printed directly from the Examiners' Copies. From 1863 to 1873. Most of the back Examination Papers may still be obtained, a few only being out of print.

EXAMINATION PAPERS IN LAW AND MODERN HISTORY. From 1866 to 1872. In One Volume, cloth, 7s. 6d.

——— IN THE SCHOOL OF NATURAL SCIENCE. From 1863 to 1868. 7s. 6d.

——— IN DISCIPLINIS MATHEMATICIS. From 1866 to 1872. 7s. 6d.

——— IN SCIENTIIS MATHEMATICIS ET PHYSICIS. From 1863 to 1868. 7s. 6d.

FOR THE YEAR 1872.

Hilary, 1872.	s.	d.	*Michaelmas*, 1872.	s.	d.
No.			No.		
147. Responsions	0	6	165. Responsions	0	6
Trinity, 1872.			163. 1st Public, Lit. Græc. et Lat.	1	0
155. Responsions	0	6	164. 1st Public, Disc. Math.	1	0
153. 1st Public, Lit. Græc. et Lat.	1	0	156. 2nd Public, Lit. Hum.	1	0
154. 1st Public, Disc. Math.	1	0	157. 2nd Public, Law and Hist.	1	0
148. 2nd Public, Lit. Hum.	1	0	160. 2nd Public, Math. et Phys.	1	0
149. 2nd Public, Law and Hist.	1	0	161. 2nd Public, Nat. Science	1	0
150. 2nd Public, Math. et Phys.	1	0	162. 2nd Public, Theology	1	0
151. 2nd Public, Nat. Science	1	0	158. 2nd Public, Modern History	1	0
152. 2nd Public, Theology	1	0	159. 2nd Public, Jurisprudence	1	0

The above are printed directly from the official copies used by the Examiners in the Schools.

PASS AND CLASS: An Oxford Guide-Book through the Courses of *Literæ Humaniores*, Mathematics, Natural Science, and Law and Modern History. By MONTAGU BURROWS, Chichele Professor of Modern History. *Third Edition.* Revised and Enlarged; with Appendices on the Indian Civil Service, the Diplomatic Service, and the Local Examinations. Fcap. 8vo., cloth, price 2s.

www.ingramcontent.com/pod-product-compliance
Lightning Source LLC
Chambersburg PA
CBHW030338170426
43202CB00010B/1169